# Cambridge Elements ≡

Elements in International Relations
edited by
Jon C. W. Pevehouse
*University of Wisconsin–Madison*
Tanja A. Börzel
*Freie Universität Berlin*
Edward D. Mansfield
*University of Pennsylvania*

Associate Editor
Jeffrey T. Checkel
*European University Institute*
Miles Kahler
*American University*

# INTERNATIONAL NORMS, MORAL PSYCHOLOGY, AND NEUROSCIENCE

Richard Price
*University of British Columbia*
Kathryn Sikkink
*Harvard University*

CAMBRIDGE
UNIVERSITY PRESS

# CAMBRIDGE
## UNIVERSITY PRESS

University Printing House, Cambridge CB2 8BS, United Kingdom

One Liberty Plaza, 20th Floor, New York, NY 10006, USA

477 Williamstown Road, Port Melbourne, VIC 3207, Australia

314–321, 3rd Floor, Plot 3, Splendor Forum, Jasola District Centre,
New Delhi – 110025, India

103 Penang Road, #05–06/07, Visioncrest Commercial, Singapore 238467

Cambridge University Press is part of the University of Cambridge.

It furthers the University's mission by disseminating knowledge in the pursuit of
education, learning, and research at the highest international levels of excellence.

www.cambridge.org
Information on this title: www.cambridge.org/9781108965972
DOI: 10.1017/9781108966610

First published 2021

*A catalogue record for this publication is available from the British Library.*

ISBN 978-1-108-96597-2 Paperback
ISSN 2515-706X (online)
ISSN 2515-7302 (print)

# International Norms, Moral Psychology, and Neuroscience

Elements in International Relations

DOI: 10.1017/9781108966610
First published online: May 2021

Richard Price
*University of British Columbia*

Kathryn Sikkink
*Harvard University*

**Author for correspondence:** Richard Price, richard.price@ubc.ca

**Abstract:** Research on international norms has yet to answer satisfactorily some of our own most important questions about the origins of norms and the conditions under which some norms win out over others. The authors argue that international relations (IR) theorists should engage more with research in moral psychology and neuroscience to advance theories of norm emergence and resonance. This Element first provides an overview of six areas of research in neuroscience and moral psychology that hold particular promise for norms theorists and international relations theory more generally. It next surveys existing literature in IR to see how literature from moral psychology is already being put to use, and then recommends a research agenda for norms researchers engaging with this literature. The authors do not believe that this exchange should be a one-way street, however, and they discuss various ways in which the IR literature on norms may be of interest and of use to moral psychologists, and of use to advocacy communities.

**Keywords:** international norms, moral psychology, neuroscience, international relations theory

ISBNs: 9781108965972 (PB), 9781108966610 (OC)
ISSNs: 2515-706X (online), 2515-7302 (print)

# Contents

# 1 Introduction

Research on international norms has advanced in very significant ways in the last several decades in the field of International Relations (IR). In our assessment, however, despite these theoretical and empirical advances, norms researchers in IR have yet to satisfactorily answer some of our own most important questions. In particular, we still have not provided sufficiently complete and thus compelling explanations for two key questions about norms. The first question is about the origins of normative beliefs, or where precisely do norms come from? The second question is about the conditions under which some normative beliefs win out over others (Finnemore and Sikkink, 1998; Florini, 1996) and begin to structure institutions and practices in world politics. By which norms win out, we are concerned not just with the conditions that lead to international institutionalization of those norms, but also those that contribute to their initial reception and implementation (Betts and Orchard, 2014). For example, many people have been surprised at the speed with which norms around LGBTQ rights have spread around the globe, even in the face of strong backlash. No new international law has been drafted, but, since 1989, when Denmark was the first to recognize civil unions for same sex couples, sixty-five countries now allow same-sex marriage or civil unions. Although 35 percent of states still criminalize same-sex relations and harsh punishment is common, twenty-six states around the world have decriminalized the practice since 2000 (ILGA, 2020). At the same time, more permissive changes in norms around refugee and migrant rights have not occurred, despite concerted efforts by advocates. The Convention on the Rights of All Migrant Workers and Members of Their Families, adopted with high hopes in 1990, has only been ratified by fifty-six states, and virtually none of these are major migrant-receiving states (United Nations Office of the High Commissioner for Human Rights, 2021). Yet norms scholars cannot persuasively explain the differences between norm changes on these two issues. Our discussion here emerges in part by way of self-critique from within the norms literature, in the sense of thinking about changes that could be made in our own work as well as those of other norms scholars.

How can theorists of normative change advance the theoretical agenda to help understand, and perhaps even do a better job, for example, of anticipating change or outcomes of various advocacy strategies? Work has begun to appear

---

We wish to thank Jeffrey Checkel and two anonymous reviewers for detailed and thoughtful comments that helped improve the manuscript greatly. We also want to thank Neta Crawford, Joshua Greene, Robert Keohane, and Dustin Tingley for comments on the manuscript, and Roshni Chakroborty and Maggie Priest for research assistance.

in recent years that investigates the implications of some of the neurological and psychological phenomena that we think holds much promise for norms research, such as the intuitive sources of morality, neurological differences between "moral tribes," advances in our understanding of empathy, as well as work that explores the implications of these phenomena for normative IR theory (Glanville, 2016, pp. 335–353; Jeffery, 2014).[1] We believe that these contributions are a promising source of insights in this enterprise and now need to be further extended. Norms in IR have largely been treated as if they are the same "thing" being considered by different agents, but once we go below the individual level into psychology and neuroscience, we find that norms may in fact be different phenomena for different types of brains. Systematic patterns are evident in brain research that holds promise in giving us leverage on why norms may resonate with distinct people in dissimilar ways.

This is not the first time constructivists have recommended a more extended engagement with research in psychology as part of the process of advancing norm theory. Katzenstein, in the conclusions to *The Culture of National Security* in 1996, suggested that "the domain of social psychology offers one possible microfoundation for studying the origins of norms" (Katzenstein, 1996a, p. 513). In 1998, Finnemore and Sikkink made a similar suggestion and pointed to psychological research on how "both cognition and affect work synergistically to produce changes in attitudes, beliefs, and preferences" (Finnemore and Sikkink, 1998, pp. 915–916). Sympathetic outsiders to constructivism made comparable recommendations. Goldgeier and Tetlock, writing a survey of psychology and international relations theory in 2001, said a cognitive psychological analysis of world politics and constructivism were compatible, but efforts to incorporate insights from cognitive science into the constructivist program were only beginning. They went on to suggest some specific research, drawing on cognitive science, to advance constructivist work (Goldgeier and Tetlock, 2001).

But these "beginnings" did not lead to a sustained research program engaging psychology and constructivism – and more specifically norm theory – with cognitive science. Finnemore, Sikkink, and Katzenstein did not follow through on their own recommendations for IR scholars to plumb psychology to address norm theory, and norm theorists, for the most part, did not take Tetlock and Goldgeier up on their suggestions for new research agendas incorporating insights from cognitive science. We will argue that the promise of a deeper dialogue between norm theory and psychology is now in the process of starting

---

[1] By "moral tribes" we refer to the term as used by Greene (2013). Among others, see especially Hall (2015); Hall and Ross (2015); Holmes (2013); Shannon (2012); Traven (2015); Wong (2016).

to be realized. The purpose of this small Element is to summarize some relevant literatures in psychology and neuroscience that we believe are of particular interest to norm theory, document the IR work underway, and signal promising directions for future research.

Political psychology is of course a rich tradition of research in political science generally and in IR, and there has been a recent explosion of interest in psychology and neuroscience (Hafner-Burton et al., 2017; Kertzer and Tingley, 2018), terrain presciently explored for many years by scholars such as Robert Jervis, Phillip Tetlock, Neta Crawford, Rose McDermott, Jonathan Mercer, and Janice Stein, among others.[2] These scholars have long recommended more dialogue between psychology and international relations, and more recently with neuroscience (McDermott, 2009).

In their 2018 survey of IR scholarship using political psychology, Kertzer and Tingley say that constructivists interact less with recent psychological work than some other parts of international relations, and suggest that "a deeper engagement between these intellectual communities will likely prove beneficial for both" (Kertzer and Tingley, 2018). McDermott and Lopez express some skepticism about the possibilities of a unified model connecting psychology and constructivism. Despite their skepticism, however, the authors suggest that incorporating psychological approaches should allow for "a clearer explanation of the origins of preferences, a puzzle that currently limits both rationalist and constructivist applications to international relations" (McDermott and Lopez, 2012, p. 197). This is exactly one of the puzzles that animates this Element, in the sense of thinking about the origins of norms. McDermott and Lopez make some proposals about incorporating insights from psychology to help constructivists theorize identity, but do not discuss norms. The Kertzer and Tingley review likewise does not mention norms research at all, underscoring the need for such an overview as we are providing in this Element.

In Section 2 we begin with a discussion of definitions of key concepts we use in the Element, and of some of the thorny epistemological and methodological issues that arise when proposing more exchanges between constructivist norm theory and psychology and neuroscience. We focus primarily on transnational norms and morality, and less on how norms and morality influence the foreign policy of an individual state, such as the United States. The study of morality and foreign policy looks at how people within a shared political culture use norms. The more puzzling question for us is how people from very different

---

[2]  See, for example, Crawford (2014, 2013); Jervis (1989); Kowert and Shannon (2012); Mattern (2011); McDermott (2009, 2004a); McDermott and Lopez (2012); Mercer (2010); Stein (1988, 2017), Tetlock (1983).

political cultures might come to agreement on particular transnational norms. This is the main topic of this Element.

We next provide in Section 3 an overview of six areas of research in neuroscience and psychology that we believe hold particular promise for norms theorists. This review may be useful as well for other IR theorists interested in applying recent theory in psychology and neuroscience to other research areas in IR. In Section 4 we survey how the literature from the brain sciences is already being put to use incorporating findings from psychology and neuroscience by researchers working on international norms. We do not believe, however, that this research has yet addressed some main unanswered questions in the existing norms literature in IR. In Section 5, we present these unanswered questions and propose prescriptions for research drawing on moral psychology and the brain sciences. This exchange with psychology should not be a one-way street, however, and in Section 5 we also discuss various ways in which the IR literature on norms may be of interest and of use to moral psychologists. In particular, we argue that the kinds of negotiation and reasoning required for the institutionalization of global norms are more responsive to some kinds of moral foundations than others, especially universal ones involving care/harm and fairness, and that other more parochial moral foundations such as loyalty, obedience, and sanctity play a more important role in sustaining existing norms, in backlash, and in blocking new norms. In Section 6 we identify practical implications of these theoretical insights including for advocacy strategies.

## 2 Definitions and Methodological Issues

### 2.1 Definitions of Key Concepts

A few working definitions of key terms are in order before proceeding with the rest of the discussion, which in due course will articulate definitions of other important concepts along the way. By norms, we refer to "collective expectations for the proper behavior of actors with a given identity" (Katzenstein, 1996b, p. 5). A key motivation of this Element has been research in psychology and neuroscience on the phenomenon of morality, and as such, this Element will focus in particular on *moral* norms.

The vast majority of the transnational norms examined in the IR literature are of moral character – norms against slavery, torture, apartheid, the use of certain weapons, and so on – but moral norms constitute a subset of the potential universe of norms. That is, some norms have relatively little if any meaningful moral content – driving either on the right side of the road or the left side, for instance.

By morality we mean what is common to many conceptualizations of morality and ethics in philosophy, normative political science including normative IR, and amongst numerous moral psychologists too – namely, ideas of what is right or wrong – "what ought we to do?" – that involve taking into consideration a concern with others.[3] We think that moral considerations are pervasive in political life including international politics,[4] and that what are often taken to be clashes between morality and self-interest (a pervasive dichotomy in IR) are often better conceptualized as conflicts between more or less parochial moralities: the interests of one's moral tribe like the nation versus a more cosmopolitan sensibility for the protection of all people against torture, for example. Kertzer et al. similarly noted what they decry as this "impoverished cleavage between realist amoralism (or immoralism) and liberal moralism" in debates about US foreign policy. Looking to test prominent moral psychologist Jonathan Haidt's moral foundations theory (which we explore in Section 3.2) with Americans' views on foreign policy, they designed a survey experiment which found that **"**What appears to liberal idealists as immoral or amoral – such as the aggressive pursuit of national security – emerges from morality as well, just of a different sort" (Kertzer et al., 2014, pp. 827–838). This is the first big takeaway from the psychological literature on morality, to realize that many sides of the debate may be morally motivated (Haidt and Joseph, 2004).

From this view, the pervasiveness of morality may make one *less* sanguine, not more, about the inevitability of conflict in human affairs and in particular IR. Moral psychologists vary in where they land on this question, with some, like Greene, believing morality in the human brain developed to solve problems within social groups, but it is an uphill battle to resolve differences among different "moral tribes." This depends upon one's view of how entrenched versus changeable moral beliefs are, and whether morally grounded positions may be held much more vehemently and zero-sum than interests which may be subject to mutually beneficial transactions – key issues we look to contribute to in this Element.[5]

---

[3] See, e.g., Greene, 2013, p. 23); the famous philosopher of global ethics Peter Singer argued "The moral point of view requires us to look beyond the interests of our own society" (Singer, 1972, p. 237); many thinkers in philosophy similarly have traditionally emphasized impartiality as central to morality, that is not simply privileging one's own interests in deciding what is right or wrong.

[4] To be sure, one can debate the extent to which even self-interestedness could be considered a moral point of view, such as libertarianism which holds individual autonomy as a moral value, but that would only expand the scope of validity of our general contention.

[5] See Tetlock on sacred versus secular values, which points to the heightened stakes of routine trade-offs involving interests versus taboo trade-offs that involve sacrificing sacred values (Tetlock et al., 2000), while also noting that many such values are pseudo-sacred and can be reframed (see Pinker (2011, pp. 622–639) .

As one part of our inquiry into morality, we are also interested in the role of emotions; not in all emotions, but in moral emotions and in moral instincts or intuitions. "Moral emotions differ from basic emotions such as fear and happiness, in that they are often linked to the interest or welfare either of society as a whole or at least of persons other than the agent."[6] Thus, we set aside the large literature on affect focused on well-being of the self, such as work on joy or anxiety, for example, and concentrate on those emotions relevant for thinking about the interests of others (Neuman, 2007). We will work with Jeffery's assessment that the "emotions are not mere feelings, but cognitive appraisals accompanied by physiological sensations," a view that is widely accepted within scholarship concerned with the emotions (Crawford, 2014; Jeffery, 2014; McDermott, 2004b). In this limited exploration, we will be dealing with ordinary emotional responses, and not extend into unique emotional and psychological issues faced by deeply traumatized populations, including epigenetic inheritance, although such issues are very relevant for scholars of postconflict societies, and thus an area of great promise for the agendas we sketch out here.[7]

Most psychologists do not share the skepticism about the role of morality in political life associated with various approaches in IR (commonly versions of realism and critical theory). These psychologists increasingly believe, as Haidt says, that human nature is "intrinsically moral," and the "human mind is designed to 'do' morality, just as it's designed to do language, sexuality, music, and many other things" (Haidt, 2012, pp. xii–xiii). Greene similarly argues that "maintaining cooperation is one of our biggest challenges. Morality is the human brain's answer to this challenge" (Greene, 2013, p. 59). Morality facilitates cooperation through "moral machinery" that operates among individuals, but also (as will also sound familiar to IR scholars) through commitments, and the emotions, promises, and threats to help us keep them; concerns with reputation, and indirect reciprocity, not just to promote self-interest, but also to punish uncooperative behavior, even at costs to ourselves. Greene sums up ample experimental data that humans are pro-social punishers with righteous indignation (Greene, 2013).

But it is still a big jump to move from saying an individual is acting at least in part out of moral considerations to the higher threshold of what IR norms scholars study – *international or transnational or even global* norms. We are interested in *transnational* moral commitments not just among states but between other actors as well, that is, an intersubjective agreement about moral

---

[6] Moll et al. (2005) citing Haidt et al. (2003).
[7] Crawford has argued that chronic stress, or even a single traumatic event may alter brains at a biochemical level (Crawford, 2014). On epigenetic inheritance, see Yehuda et al. (2016).

values across borders of states. Hafner-Burton and her colleagues have referred to this as the "aggregation issue" – how to move from studying individual to collective decision-making (Hafner-Burton et al., 2017, p. S5). These different concerns mean that we must be cautious about how we incorporate findings in moral psychology into norms theory, but also implies that IR norms theory may have something interesting to contribute to the larger debates in moral psychology.

## 2.2 Epistemological and Methodological Concerns

Some of our readers may wonder if we (two self-described social constructivist IR scholars) are delving into the neuroscience of moral norms to offer some variant of biological determinism or essentialism.[8] But while there have been a variety of approaches that more directly tie human morality to biology such as the field of sociobiology, we are far from offering such natural determinism. We believe we need to be cautious about how we use neuroscience, and yet at the same time we believe we can no longer advance our understanding of emotions or morality or norms without some discussion of neuroscience and psychology.[9]

Although we explore the implications of the findings that much of morality may be driven by automatic intuitions, many of which arise as embodied emotions such as disgust or empathy, we are not reducing all morality to emotion nor intuitions. It is very important not to move from an overly rational understanding of moral reasoning to one that rests solely on emotion. In terms of the relationship between emotion and reason, the latest research on emotion suggests that emotion organizes or facilitates rationality rather than replaces it, and this is where we situate our work (Crawford, 2014; Verweij et al., 2015).

We suggest that one reason that constructivists and norm theorists took so long to follow through on the dialogue with psychology also had to do with differences between much of social science and psychology more generally, as well as with internal disputes within constructivism about epistemology and method. Constructivism has historically tended to share with much of social science, including much of political science, the view that human behavior is powerfully shaped by the external environment and by socialization. The strongest version of "this perspective – variably dubbed 'cultural determinism' (e.g., Alcock, 2001), the 'standard social science model' (e.g., Barkow et al.,

---

[8]  That would place us in the company of a number of IR scholars working with critical and post-structural perspectives who have in their analyses of emotions engaged the relevance of the body. See Hutchinson's (2016) comprehensive review of the literature.

[9]  Tingley argues that resistance to evolutionary thought in political science is "largely the legacy of one error, the naturalistic fallacy, whereby an 'is' of nature becomes an 'ought' of morality, as it did notoriously in Social Darwinism and the Eugenics Movement" (Tingley, 2006, p. 23).

1995), or, more popularly, the 'blank slate' (e.g., Pinker 2002) – views the mind as wholly molded by the cultural environment and without any 'built-in' biological tendencies"(Horowitz et al., 2014). Because of its very identity as an approach concerned with social construction of politics, constructivism may be even more wedded to the blank-slate model than other approaches in IR (McDermott and Lopez, 2012) – "ideas all the way down" in Wendt's memorable phrase (even as Wendt himself granted a reality constraint at some point). Some constructivists may have endorsed the blank-slate model (though usually not explicitly) because of its progressive philosophical appeal and the fear of biological determination with its potential for racism and sexism (Pinker, 2002).[10] But the findings we review below suggest that a blank-slate view of human nature cannot be sustained in the light of research advances *and* that engaging with psychology does not imply biological determinism. A key intended contribution here is to identify complementarities of the variety of different methodologies of IR and neuroscience and moral psychology, but also to assess where those different approaches may point in disparate directions or make different contributions.

The internal disputes within constructivism about the appropriate means for establishing truth claims took many forms, but at times, the possibility of using science itself was called into question, and much ink was spilled over whether and how constructivist researchers could use positivist methods. As will be more than evident from the title and content of this Element and the Introduction, we situate ourselves within a group of modern constructivists who believe that interpretation and science are mutually compatible, and that research on the material world can and does inform our understanding of nonmaterial phenomena like norms.

But other significant differences also separate psychological and constructivist views of human behavior (McDermott and Lopez, 2012, p. 197). Much of the literature of moral emotions and intuitions, especially that which draws on neuroscience, is concerned with the micro, while norms theorists are interested in broad intersubjective macro trends or normative change in the world (Crawford, 2013). Perhaps because of this, work in IR using psychology and neurobiology has tended to focus on individual-level research, especially leadership, foreign policy decision-making, and violence.[11] The attention may be directed to the traits of exceptional individuals or outliers with regard to their

---

[10] Pinker discusses four fears that may keep many progressives from accepting any biological explanations: the fear of inequality, imperfectability, determinism, and nihilism.

[11] See McDermott and Hatemi, for example, who focus on leadership and political violence (Mcdermott and Hatemi, 2014). See also Hafner-Burton et al. (2017).

capacity for violence, rather than how normal human brains program ordinary people.

Criticisms of the relevance of psychological experiments and surveys for the real world of global politics are well rehearsed and while they will not be summarized and repeated at length here, we very much underscore the need for such cautions to be heeded. Many of the findings in neuroscience spurring our interest have been driven both by experiments and by the use of new technological techniques for studying brains, in particular functional magnetic resonance imaging (fMRI) scans and what they tell us about how brains process morality. Although neuroimaging of cognition was well advanced in the 1990s, the first brain imaging studies of moral judgments were reported as recently as 2001, so the field of the neuroscience of moral beliefs is relatively new (Sinnott-Armstrong, 2007, p. xiii). This tool has been very useful, but is still in development and has a number of limitations.[12] McDermott argues that one limitation of fMRI research is that is only informs observers about the place in the brain where activation occurs, not the actual mental processes that are of most interest to researchers (McDermott, 2009, p. 579). But some moral psychologists like Poldrack argue that while reverse inference is challenging, fMRI has helped understand how different brain regions provide us with cognitive abilities (Poldrack, 2018). Tingley offers a different critique of fMRI, arguing that it cannot reach beyond description to help social scientists test competing theoretical explanations. As a result, Tingley recommends an approach to the use of neurological data that emphasizes comparative theoretical testing. He also reminds us of how many unsettled disputes continue in the neuroscience area, some of which we will discuss (Tingley, 2011).

There has been increasing interest in microfoundations in IR over the past twenty years, but "a surprising lack of specificity" about what they are (Kertzer, 2017). Our purpose is not just to talk about the need for microfoundations for norms theory, but to start specifying what some of those might be, in light of the findings about morality and emotions like empathy from recent waves of research. Some constructivists may eschew an emphasis on microfoundations because it implies strong methodological individualism. Although we recognize that there are some IR questions that do not lend themselves to a study of microfoundations (Kertzer, 2017, p. 84; Wendt, 1999), we believe that many aspects of norm theory are not only amenable to such an approach but may require it to advance theory building. It is likely that this research will be of more interest to scholars working in a tradition of agentic constructivism,

---

[12] See, e.g., Poldrack (2018). See also, discussions of the limitation of fMRI technology in McDermott (2009); Tingley (2011, 2006). Thank you to Marika Landau-Wells for her guidance in this regard.

focused on emergence of new norms and norm entrepreneurship, rather than more structural versions of constructivism concerned more with well-established logics of appropriateness.[13]

## 3 Overview of Relevant Theory and Findings from the Neuroscience and Psychology of Moral Intuitions and Reason

We begin with an overview of some of the major categories of contributions from psychology and neuroscience that offer promising insights for norm theory.

### 3.1 The Dual Processing Brain

Numerous psychologists have made the case that the human mind has two largely distinct processing systems, a view made most famous perhaps by Daniel Kahneman's pithy characterization of our abilities for "thinking fast and slow" (Kahneman, 2011). According to this view, our cognition is driven by two largely distinct processes or systems: an automatic, intuitive system that takes place without conscious invocation or even awareness, and a slower, effortful system of reasoned deliberation. Neurological studies show that because slow reasoning takes much more time, intuitions are the default for most people most of the time to economize cognitive effort (Kahneman, 2011). Intuitions, a key concept for this Element, are "the judgments, solutions, and ideas that pop into consciousness *without our being aware* of the mental processes that led to them" (Haidt and Joseph, 2004, p. 56; emphasis added). Kahneman importantly noted that it is the effortful processes of rational deliberation that we associate with the subjective experience of agency, choice, and concentration; these processes act as a complementary modulatory control system (Kahneman, 2011, chap. 1). While not at all without controversy, the research evidence for the dual process brain is now very substantial, as are the results of fMRI studies that suggest these processing systems appear to be controlled from different parts of the brain.[14]

Some IR theorists, following Kahneman, refer to an intuitive and emotional "System 1" and a slow-moving rational "System 2," that in their mind approximates rational choice. In this version, the inappropriate selection of heuristics and emotions associated with System 1, is often seen as distorting rational judgment, frequently to the detriment of good policy (Hafner-Burton et al., 2017). Greene suggests a somewhat different and more fruitful understanding in his analogy between the dual processing human brain and a camera with

---

[13] On agentic and structural constructivism, see Sikkink (2011, pp. 235–237).
[14] See, e.g., Jost et al. (2014, pp. 7–8); Miller and Cohen (2001).

automatic settings and manual settings. For many circumstances, the automatic settings on a camera are useful, fast, and efficient. But there are more complicated moments when we need to override the automatic settings and move to the manual mode to get more flexibility, which is more time consuming and effortful (Greene, 2013). This manual setting is capable of rational choice thinking, but not limited to it; it is also able to engage in moral reasoning.

Haidt offered the important clarification that once he stopped thinking in terms of emotion versus cognition and "started thinking about *intuition versus reasoning,* everything fell into place" (Haidt, 2012, p. 46; emphasis added). In other words, intuition and reasoning are two different kinds of cognition (Haidt, 2012, p. 45). IR theorists drawing on psychology who think the dual processing brain is about emotion versus rational choice would be well advised to take note of this distinction. Throughout this Element we will highlight this understanding of the dual process brain – that of a fast automatic mode of intuitions, emotions, and heuristics and a slower manual mode of reasoning. Reasoning "involves the conscious application of decision rules," (Greene, 2014, p. 136) but those rules do not at all have to be rational choice rules, nor do they have to be the utilitarian rules that Greene proposes. Reasoning also can involve moral reasoning based, for example, on deontological or legal decision rules.

Psychologists do not share the common social science view that emotion mainly impedes reasoning. Psychological research has revealed that "reasoning cannot produce good decisions without some kind of emotional input" (Greene, 2013, p. 46). This is clear from neuroscientist Antonio Damasio's famous patient "Elliot," who lost part of his brain's frontal lobe while having surgery to remove a tumor. As a result of the surgery, Elliot's brain could no longer connect reason and emotion. He still had a very high IQ, but he was incapable of making decisions (Damasio, 1994). Clearly emotion can bias our thinking, but better thinking, or arguing, does not come from a complete lack of emotion. "Emotion helps us screen, organize and prioritize the information that bombards us. It influences what information we find salient, relevant, convincing or memorable" (Bandes and Salerno, 2014, p. 1011).[15]

Greene (2014, p. 294) argues that moral intuitions offer reasonably good advice for the basic problem of cooperation within a "moral tribe" ("Me vs. Us"), but offers unreliable advice concerning disagreements between and among tribes with competing interests and values ("Us vs. Them"). The instinctive *us vs. them* response of the brain can be unconscious and fast, and also can happen at a very young age. For example, monolingual children show in-group biases not only for individuals who speak their native language, but

---

[15] See also, Verweij et al. (2015).

also for people who speak it without a foreign accent (Kinzler et al., 2007). Such intuitive ability to detect in-groups and out-groups may be the basis for discriminatory and othering behavior seen in so much of the world, including the rise of anti-immigrant sentiments. Such findings do not validate racism as somehow inherent, in part because conflict among moral tribes in our evolutionary history usually did not involve racial differences. Rather, "race, far from being an innate trigger, is just something that we happen to use today as a marker of group membership" (Greene, 2013, p. 52).

These findings may also be quite relevant to helping us think about norms research, and yet, to do so, we both draw on and part paths from Greene and some of the theorists of moral intuitions. Presumably, most of international relations, using Greene's terms, is concerned with "us vs. them." We argue that moral intuitions are useful in helping explain the origins and transnational resonance of norms, but that not all moral intuitions lend themselves equally to being institutionalized as global norms.

Greene believes that deontological claims about rights that are seen as "natural" are almost solely a product of moral intuitions (e.g., about harm and fairness), not of reasoning, and thus are easier to make than the hard trade-offs required by utilitarian thought. This may be the case when thinking about an individual's intuitions, but it is unlikely to be true for the processes of deliberation leading to transnational or global norms. So, for example, the initial intuitions that social movements brought to and utilized in their advocacy on landmines may have relied on appealing to the public's automatic mode, concerned with maimed civilians harmed by indiscriminate mines. But when diplomats met to negotiate a treaty against landmines, they needed to move to the manual mode to formulate persuasive and explicit arguments about why other governments should favor multiple provisions of such a treaty (Price, 1998).

## 3.2 Moral Intuitions and Moral Foundations Theory (MFT)

One key motivation of this Element was the critical secondary claim that has followed from this bifurcated view of our cognitive processing system: the case championed by Haidt and colleagues that "moral intuitions arise automatically and almost instantaneously, long before moral reasoning has a chance to get started, and those first intuitions tend to drive our later reasoning" (Haidt, 2012, p. xiv). Renee Jeffery has pointed out that there is a parallel between this view of moral intuitions and the moral sentiment theory of the Scottish Enlightenment, most importantly David Hume, who argued that human beings have a moral sense of right and wrong that guides ethical reasoning. Jeffery (2014) further argues for a sentimentalist cosmopolitan approach that recognizes that emotions are essential for ethical reasoning, and that they can yield outcomes that are not selfish.

Haidt's approach, which in turn builds on earlier research, is not accepted by all moral psychologists. A variety of methods of experimental psychology, cross-cultural surveys, and cognitive neuroscience, however, have provided sufficient evidence for Haidt's claims that they are well worth reflecting upon for our findings in IR regarding moral norms. Other moral psychologists have and will put forward different models of morality and ideology worth exploring (Duckitt and Sibley, 2010; Janoff-Bulman and Carnes, 2013; Schwartz, 2012; Schwartz et al., 2010). We focus here on moral intuitions and moral foundations theory because we have found these to be particularly promising for IR research on norms

Psychologists have used extensive survey and fMRI research to illuminate what Steven Pinker called "the moral instinct," and what Haidt and his colleagues call the five foundations of morality: (1) care/harm, (2) fairness/cheating, (3) loyalty/betrayal, (4) authority/subversion, and (5) sanctity/degradation (Graham et al., 2013; Haidt, 2012; Pinker, 2008). This literature is often linked together under the label of "Moral Foundations Theory," or MFT, created by a group of psychologists to understand "why morality varies so much across cultures yet still shows so many similarities and recurrent themes."[16] MFT discusses the aforementioned five moral foundations for which they have the most evidence, and a sixth "good candidate for foundationhood,": liberty/oppression. These six categories have been broken down into three that they characterize as *individualizing* foundations: care, fairness, and liberty, and three that are called *binding* foundations because they are about the protection of the group or institution by binding individuals into roles or duties: loyalty, authority, and sanctity.[17] Moral foundations theorists argue that their work is descriptive, not normative, in the sense that it describes how morality actually works in the brain, rather than how it should work (Graham et al., 2013).

MFT researchers have produced evidence that these foundations are common across cultures. But contrary to essentializing narratives that depict countries or civilizations as having distinctive moral values, it is actually *within* cultures that these scholars see the greatest variability, namely between those who embrace the more individualizing foundations and those who support the binding foundations. Binding foundations speak more to

---

[16] See https://moralfoundations.org/.
[17] Others argue the main animating divide between individualizing and binding moral foundation is between concern and definition of the in-group; see Graham et al. (2013).

conservatives and individualizing ones are those that resonate more strongly with liberals and libertarians, as these terms are used in the United States. MFT finds that liberals tend to put more moral weight on values like preventing harm and enforcing fairness (understood in terms of equality), while conservatives give more weight to in-group loyalty, sanctity, and authority. Thus, a message that might appeal to one type of brain could backfire for another. Conservatives do not necessarily discount fairness altogether, nor protection from harm (see, e.g., pro-life movements), but those are only two along with the other moral foundations that tend to prevail. Moreover, conservatives tend to have a different conception of fairness understood as just deserts, whereas liberals tend to gravitate toward fairness as greater equality (Haidt, 2012). This may account for a finding by Feinberg and Willer, further exploring MFT, that "conservatism is based fundamentally on the acceptance and legitimation of inequality, and the willingness to prioritize the ingroup's goals over the welfare of those in the outgroup" (Feinberg and Willer, 2015). The sixth "candidate" for a moral foundation, liberty/oppression, is associated with libertarianism. Finally, both liberals and conservatives believe that it is appropriate to punish norm transgressors, but differ with regard to the form that this punishment should take.

While most of these moral foundations will be familiar to the reader (see Figure 1) perhaps the most novel contribution that MFT makes is to remind us of the ongoing moral importance in the world of the intuitive sanctity/degradation foundation, also referred to as concerns about purity, that are shaped by the psychology of disgust and contamination. Such a sanctity moral

1) **Care/harm**: This foundation is related to our long evolution as mammals with attachment systems and an ability to feel (and dislike) the pain of others. It underlies virtues of kindness, gentleness, and nurturance.

2) **Fairness/cheating**: This foundation is related to the evolutionary process of reciprocal altruism. It generates ideas of justice, rights, and autonomy, and includes concerns about equality and proportionality.

3) **Loyalty/betrayal:** This foundation is related to our long history as tribal creatures able to form shifting coalitions. It underlies virtues of patriotism and self-sacrifice for the group. It is active anytime people feel that it's "one for all, and all for one."

4) **Authority/subversion:** This foundation was shaped by our long primate history of hierarchical social interactions. It underlies virtues of leadership and followership, including deference to legitimate authority and respect for traditions.

5) **Sanctity/degradation:** This foundation was shaped by the psychology of disgust and contamination. It underlies religious notions of striving to live in an elevated, less carnal, more noble way. It underlies the widespread idea that the body is a temple which can be desecrated by immoral activities and contaminants (an idea not unique to religious traditions).

6) **Liberty/oppression:** This foundation is about the feelings of reactance and resentment people feel toward those who dominate them and restrict their liberty. Its intuitions are often in tension with those of the authority foundation. The hatred of bullies and dominators motivates people to come together, in solidarity, to oppose or take down the oppressor.

**Figure 1** Moral foundations; https://moralfoundations.org/

foundation is found in many religious beliefs, but is not unique to them. Some modern secular vegetarians, for example, are not only motivated by a concern with harming animals, but also by a strong reaction of disgust to the idea of eating animal flesh, which suggests the presence of a purity foundation. Extreme concern about the spread of infectious diseases such as Ebola or coronavirus may be provoked not only by the care/harm foundation, but also by fear of contamination. Anyone who thinks that they are immune from the moral foundation of sanctity should go the MFT website and take the "disgust scale" questionnaire.[18]

This literature does not provide a simple answer to which "issue characteristics" will be most influential in the emergence of new norms but does suggest that there are some generalizable patterns in moral reasoning. Both Haidt and other researchers have found evidence for similar categories and patterns of moral reasoning in research conducted in a wide range of countries around the world. The implications for norms research and for moral advocacy in world politics are far-reaching.

Issues in international politics may invoke a range of different moral intuitions, often in contrasting ways. Images of refugees fleeing war and crisis can generate concerns about harm, and about fairness, in terms of our desire, for example, to treat immigrants coming from Muslim countries in a nondiscriminatory manner. But strong intuitions about loyalty to in-groups and fear about terrorism contribute to a desire to exclude out-groups. In contrast to the powerful emotions that may arise from intuitive reactions to such events, research on the effortful systems of the brain help us understand that immigration amounts to a "brutal workout for the brain, culture shock is brain shock" (Doidge, 2007, p. 298) and thus the reception of foreign peoples is not something that comes easily if at all for many people given that our System 2 is lazy and many people avoid cognitive effort as much as possible (Kahneman, 2011, p. 45).

Haidt and numerous colleagues emphasize the primacy of the intuitive and are more skeptical of the role typically played by deliberative reasoning in moral positions; others, like Greene, largely share this view but grant more of a role for the possibility of reasoned deliberation, particularly with utilitarian types of judgments. Still, even the foremost proponent of the intuitionist account concedes that reasoned persuasion can occur. As Haidt concisely puts it, "Intuitions come first and reasoning is usually produced after a judgment is made, in order to influence other people. But as a discussion progresses, the reasons given by other people sometimes change our intuitions and judgments" (Haidt, 2012, p. 47). His scheme is exemplified in his model in Figure 2:

---

[18] www.yourmorals.org/explore.php.

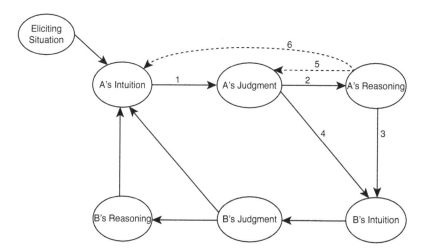

**Figure 2** Haidt's Social Intuitionist model

These diverse ways of understanding how human brains actually process morality raises some immediate implications for how IR scholars have understood norms. For one, what IR scholars have often taken to be the chief evidence for moral concern in world politics – reasoned reflection, then argumentation and persuasion, represented in lines 5 and 3 in Figure 2 – is seen by prominent moral psychologists like Haidt to be largely a distraction as moral arguments are "mostly post hoc constructions made up on the fly" (Haidt, 2012, p. xiv).

There are plenty of critiques by psychologists about MFT; we consider but a few here of particular interest. Narvaez, for example, criticizes intuitionist approaches to morality like MFT as incomplete, because "intuition and reasoning are constitutive, interactive, and educable" in the moral domain (Narvaez, 2010, p. 164). Indeed, Graham, Haidt and their MFT colleagues agreed that "Narvaez is correct that we have focused too much of our attention on the initial moral judgment, and not enough on the processes by which morality develops and improves with experience" (Graham et al., 2013, p. 33). Narvaez goes on to argue that "moral intuitionist theories often seem to rely on data from novices using seat-of-the-pants intuition – a quick, prereflective, front-end intuition that novices typically display" (Narvaez, 2010, p. 171). This is quite relevant for scholars of international relations, because many actors in world politics are not novices in the area of moral reasoning, and thus it is useful to ask whether MFT offers incomplete microfoundations for understanding these more seasoned actors operating in iterative multilateral fora, a topic we discuss at more length in Section 4.

Proponents of MFT, however, defend themselves, clarifying that for them, "innate means *organized in advance of experience*" … not hardwired or insensitive to environmental influences (Graham et al., 2013, p. 8; emphasis added). These moral intuitions provide, as Haidt says, the "taste buds of the righteous mind" (Haidt, 2012, p.112). Just as individuals have the same taste buds but very different preferences in food, they do not explain simple uniformity. Likewise, as research on very young toddlers and other primates has revealed, the desire to help others and a concern with harm is not only the result of parent's moral training, but a natural behavior that appears before language and across cultures (Bloom, 2013; Warneken and Tomasello, 2006, pp. 1301–1303).

## 3.3 Gene–Culture Coevolution/Dual Inheritance Theory

One approach that would appear particularly useful for constructivist norm theory is the gene–culture evolution theory, also called dual inheritance theory (DIT), because it focuses on genetic and cultural evolution as two different and interacting processes. Boyd and Richerson laid down the theoretical foundations of this approach in their 1985 book, *Culture and the Evolutionary Process* (Boyd and Richerson, 1985). DIT takes culture, learning, and social norms very seriously. Because its focus is more on cultures than individuals, it also may be a better fit with international norms theory than the more individualistic approach of MFT. The general frame of DIT is very consistent with the approach we advocate here, because it explores the ways that culture and norms have shaped innate psychology to enhance the abilities of humans to cooperate in larger groups. DIT affirms many propositions of existing norm theory, including the importance of the prestige, success, or "prominence" of norm entrepreneurs who propose norms, the role of imitation and conformity in norm transmission, as well as the crucial role of third parties to sanction norm violations (Finnemore and Sikkink, 1998; Florini, 1996). Gene–culture coevolution sees norms mainly as transmitted through imitation and conformism (Gintis, 2007), not through social learning and the kinds of deliberation that IR theorists have also emphasized.

The work in this field has been driven by the very longue durée of human evolution, and has relied on mathematical models of the evolution of social learning under different environmental conditions such as that of Boyd and Richerson. More recent work by Joseph Henrich and colleagues is more accessible and relevant, but equally confined to long term processes of human evolution that led to the emergence of social norms. The characterization of norms in this work is quite similar to that in IR norms research, focused on "concerns for reputation, internalization of norms, pro-social biases, and shame and anger at norms violators" (Henrich, 2015, p. 60). DIT provides a useful general framework similar to the one we propose here that takes both evolution and culture and norms seriously.

But this remarkable convergence begins to dissipate as we look more closely at the actual research of DIT which is primarily concerned with social norms around issues like monogamous marriage, food taboos, naming practices, and kin relations, not the kinds of social norms that might maintain harmony in international politics (Henrich, 2015, pp. 154 & 215). In this model, similar to the argument proposed by Greene, pro-social norms emerged under the influence of intergroup competition, since norms that increased cooperation within a group gave it an advantage vis-à-vis other groups that lacked such norms (Henrich, 2015, p. 167).

Because the kinds of norms used in DIT models evolve so slowly in distinct cultural groups and dissipate when different cultures come too much in contact with one another, it is not clear yet how the approach could be used to generate specific hypotheses about the emergence and resonance of transnational norms. There are however, some examples of general hypotheses from this literature that may be relevant for the emergence or resonance of some transnational norms as opposed to others. Henrich (2015) proposes that "social norms are especially strong and enduring when they hook into our innate psychology. For example, social norms for fairness toward foreigners will be much harder to spread and sustain than those that demand mothers care for their children" (p. 330). However, Henrich's list of the kinds of norms that "hook into our innate psychology," aside from "favoritism to close kin and preferences for reciprocity," are generally less relevant to politics, such as "aversion to incest, readiness to avoid meat, and desire for pair-bonding" (p. 330). Henrich also explores the impact of intergroup competition on norms; in particular, the impact of war on social norms and cooperation. Using experiments involving games like the Public Goods Game and the Dictator Game, DIT researchers found that people from communities that had experienced more war-related violence were more likely to cooperate with fellow villagers, and experienced strengthened social norms and more tightly bonded communities (p. 207).[19] But the relevance of this hypothesis is unclear with regard to transnational norms. In general, the DIT literature, like Greene's moral psychology, helps explain why social norms and morality are important to increasingly large communities, up to and including the nation-state. But it falls short, as we see, in helping IR scholars understand the role of transnational social norms in relations among states.

---

[19] Presaging our later discussion of empathy, see also Hartman and Morse (2020) who argue that past exposure to violence increases individuals' capacity to empathize with others, which motivates helping behavior toward members of different ethnic or religious groups.

## 3.4 Political Neuroscience: The Politics of Brains

The literature on moral foundations of liberals and conservatives is connected to related work in political neuroscience. Both have arrived at the idea that different people have different kinds of brains, but while MFT theory works with a quite small number of moral intuitions, political neuroscience highlights a wider range of ways in which liberals and conservatives differ.

Drawing on the work of Oxley et al. and many others, Jost and colleagues have coined the term "political neuroscience" for the field, which they date from about 2003. Political neuroscience has been characterized by the use of neuroscientific methods to analyze questions of political psychology such as electroencephalography (EEG), fMRI, and other measures of the central and peripheral nervous system to examine evidence of the neural bases of ideological positions. They demonstrate that there is "abundant evidence" in their own work and in the literature that "liberals and conservatives differ in terms of uncontrolled *physiological* responses to stimuli, brain function, and even static brain anatomy" (Jost et al., 2014; Oxley et al., 2008). The findings include, among others: conservatives exhibit preferences for stability, tradition, duty, and command, whereas liberals exhibit preferences for opposite values, such as flexibility, progress, compromise, diversity, and feminism. Personal needs for order, structure, and cognitive closure as well as personal sensitivity to dangerous and threatening stimuli and needs to manage fear and anxiety are in turn positively associated with resistance to change, acceptance of inequality, system justification, and political conservatism. Liberal, relative to conservative, thinking is related to greater cognitive flexibility, more empathy, and less concern with fear.[20]

New research has called some of these claims into question, particularly those that argue that liberals and conservatives have different physiological responses to threats. Bakker and his coauthors reveal that they were unable to replicate findings by Oxley and his lab (2008) that conservatives have greater physiological responses to threat, an important finding for the field of political neuroscience. Bakker et al. do not call into question the "robust" connection between political ideology and *self-reported* perceptions of threat, but they cannot find a physical manifestation of it. As a result, they "reject the foundational assumption of the work conducted by Oxley et al." (Bakker et al., 2020). They end with a proviso that echoes our approach here:

> We do not think that this should be the end of the biology and politics theory Oxley et al. helped initiate. Other fields have found that while the structure of

---

[20] See Jost et al. (2014).

the brain affects human behaviour, it does not do so in direct and easily measured ways. Politics should be no different, especially given the complex personal experiences that politics evokes. (Bakker et al., 2020, p. 616)

The way liberal and conservative are used in such research may raise worries in IR that they are being understood and deployed in an essentializing fashion, as if these are not contestable concepts but instead objective natural kinds, let alone changeable themselves within individuals.[21] This bears scrutiny by political scientists in fruitful conversation with psychologists to be sure. We should be wary of taking these differences as static moral positions, that one is born liberal or conservative and that people are just different. This has been abetted by popular impressions of innate differences on issues like climate change between political tribes, divides that some studies have suggested can actually be accentuated by appeals to evidence as people dig themselves more into established positions even in the face of evidence contrary to their views (Mercier and Sperber, 2017; Sloman and Fernbach, 2017). Indeed, such connotations are implied by the very way some have defined moral intuitions as "strong, stable, immediate moral beliefs" which often resist counterevidence (Sinnott-Armstrong et al., 2010, p. 246).

Still, findings about differences even between self-reported conservative and liberal political temperaments provide us with useful evidence about conflicting moral inclinations issuing from tendencies toward reform or more radical change, order, fear, and complexity, among others. What they do not tell us is how macro change happens, that is, the context of what counts as preserving the existing order in one time, but what was in fact change in another. Few conservatives today are willing to explicitly justify slavery, while many in the United States would have 150 years ago. IR research has shown attitudes can become codified in norms over time, and embedded in institutions. In turn, powerful norms, reinforced by law, provide limits to the moral imagination.

## 3.5 Neuroplasticity and Change

Another related issue here then is the extent to which such moral positions are subject to change, and which ways the causal arrows point in terms of sources of morality. Jost and colleagues summarize that:

The most common view is that physiological and psychological characteristics (including personality traits) are heritable, stable, and difficult to change, and so they must shape political dispositions, rather than the other way around. This overarching assumption has led some to conclude, quite erroneously, that social and political outcomes (such as racism and political

---

[21] On natural kinds from a scientific realist perspective, see Wendt (1999).

orientation) are "hard-wired ... . Political orientation, we submit, is the product of an "elective affinity" between the discursive, socially constructed elements of ideological belief systems and the psychological constraints, motives, and interests of those who are drawn to those belief systems, so that ... not only do people choose ideas, but "ideas choose people." (Jost et al., 2014, p. 29)

Most neuroscientists are thus not forwarding either a biological determinist nor static argument about morality, but a more subtle constitutive one with a role for experience, culture, socialization, learning and deliberation, as well as strategic interaction (Tingley, 2006). Even so, those working in the natural sciences may have too thin an account of these factors, and in particular of the political.[22] The political is much more than individuals who are right and left, liberal and conservative, and this is exactly an area where there are possibilities for productive exchanges between political science and psychology in IR. We propose thicker ways of understanding politics that can lead to different expectations. To engage in this exchange, however, political scientists need to understand that these psychologists are *not* saying that the brain is "hard-wired" and thus fixed and immutable, but both "prewired" and yet plastic, that is, with certain predispositions, and yet capable of and subject to change (Marcus, 2004, p. 12). When Joshua Greene wrote that "our brains are wired for tribalism" he immediately hastened to add "that being wired for tribalism does not mean being *hardwired* for tribalism. Brains can be *rewired* [emphasis added] through experience and active learning" (Greene, 2013, p. 55).

Neuroplasticity is a term used to convey the idea that brain's structure and function can change through thought and activity, and indeed that the brain is constantly doing so even in older humans rather than just younger people as they develop. The ongoing activities of our brains are characterized by competitive plasticity – that is, when it comes to allocating brain processing power, brain maps are governed by competition for precious resources and the principle of use it or lose it: "if we stop exercising mental skills, we don't just forget them: the brain map space for those skills is turned over to the skills we practice instead" (Doidge, 2007, p. 59). We are convinced that findings about how adaptable the brain is have importance for thinking about transnational norms.

Interestingly, Narvaez underscores that we can learn through experience in ways that are often not self-conscious: "As a result of implicit learning through these systems, the effects of prior experiences are manifest in a task even though previous learning is not consciously evident to the performer . . . . What we often

---

[22] Tingley argues that "evolutionary psychology, and evolutionary theory more generally, leaves out the political part of culture and thus does not offer a robust account of culture" (Tingley, 2006, p. 28).

call 'understanding' belongs to the sophisticated unconscious, implicit aware-ness, such that we know more than we can explain" (Narvaez, 2010, p. 167). Dedicated training too can alter our intuitions, which "develop from immersion and extensive, focused practice" (Narvaez, 2010, p. 171).

All this is highly suggestive, both of moral practice in general, and the enactment of more specific beliefs into behavior and how such behavior may in turn *change our intuitions* by literally changing our brains. Does this mean then that those with predominantly parochial moralities can become cosmopol-itans with sufficient education and/or experience? What would that take? Conversely, what accounts for the lack of uptake or even backlash to the spread of various liberal internationalist/cosmopolitan ideas such as generosity toward refugees or LGTBQ rights?

For one, findings in brain plasticity are not meant to imply that humans are always actually changing even as that latent possibility may exist. The "plastic paradox" is that anything that involves unvaried repetition can lead to rigidity; neuroplasticity is best thought of "like pliable snow on a hill. When we go down the hill on a sled, we can be flexible . . . but if we choose the same path a second or third time, tracks will start to develop, and soon we will tend to get stuck in a rut" (Doidge, 2007, p. 242). Other factors can contribute to declines in plasticity which in turn may help explain political developments: seeking out like-minded individuals, or ignoring or discrediting information that does not match beliefs. Moreover, when there seems to be a mismatch between develop-ments in the world and our preferred moral outcomes, as we grow older we tend to try to control the world to make it familiar, rather than change ourselves. Some psychologists thereby attribute cross-cultural conflict to such relative decreases in plasticity (Wexler, 2006). So, for example, the perceived influx of novel and strange peoples and their customs brought on by immigration might be extremely challenging to some brains (Doidge, 2007, p. 298).

Some, like Jost, are less dismissive than other authors of the possibility that "political attitudes [could] shift a person's general emotional dispositions . . ." so "we would hypothesize that certain ideological narratives or frames, if they are consistently encountered and embraced, could indeed affect the individual's psychological and physiological characteristics."[23] So, neural plasticity pro-vides a critical mechanism of how people with given predispositions can change individually. But, while the brain is shaped by social and cultural relations, such changes are not boundless. Neuroplasticity must be understood as operating within limits (Verweij et al., 2015, p. 5). Neuroplasticity thus offers both opportunities and challenges to constructivism, to understand both how these

---

[23] Jost et al. (2014), p. 308 (first quotation citing Hibbing et al., in press, p. 27).

moments of change happen, and also the limits to such change. We should not be surprised, for example, about backlash to cosmopolitan norms, given human prewiring for relations among smaller groups. "Because the plastic brain can always allow brain functions that it has brought together to separate, a regression to barbarism is always possible, and civilization will always be a tenuous affair that must be taught in each generation and is always, at most, one generation deep" (Doidge, 2007, p. 298). This is a claim full of implications for thinking about the location and durability of normative structures. IR scholars have identified a number of mechanisms by which norms can become entrenched – such as institutionalization in domestic law, in international law and international institutions, and in practices – which produces constituencies with interests and commitments to those rules (Adler and Pouliot, 2011; Crawford, 2014). Scholars of "norm contestation," have determined that the transnational norms they studied remained robust despite direct challenges, in part because they were embedded in institutions and law (Deitelhoff and Zimmermann, 2019, p. 2). We completely agree that people need to be vigilant about defending cosmopolitan norms, but the political possibilities of both domestic and international institutionalization of such norms may make the situation somewhat less tenuous than a complete refresh from the ground up required of each generation insofar as institutional effects scaffold on top of each other.

## 3.6 Empathy and Altruism

Advances in our understanding of empathy is yet another major area in the brain sciences with important implications for IR scholars studying norms. Contrary to long-dominant assumptions of the self-interestedness of human nature in social sciences like economics and also political science, it is more accurate to view humans as a species that evolved by being wired for pro-social behavior. In an early discussion of the implications of empathy for international relations, Keohane considered the possibilities of "empathetic interdependence," when actors could be interested in the welfare of others for its own sake, and learn to think about their interests in ways that incorporate empathy (Keohane, 1984). From the point of view of moral psychology, empathy "may be the most quintessentially moral feature of our brains," (Greene, 2013, p. 264) and is widely perceived across numerous fields as a key to humanitarian behavior. The implications are potentially momentous, since as Jeremy Rifkin asked in a more popular treatment, if human civilizations have been able to transcend past socially constructed parochial blood ties and the like characterized by enmity, is it really such a stretch to foresee further expanding our empathic concern

(Rifkin, 2009)? For noted philosopher Peter Singer, the project of global ethics is fundamentally one of widening the circle of empathy, which, in his account, reason has been able to gradually accomplish over time beyond the initial origins of empathy as a genetically based drive to protect one's kin (Singer, 2011, see also Crawford, 2009). Indeed, if morality is as pervasive in politics as the research we are drawing from suggests, then understanding more about the capacity to expand one's concern for others emerges as a central concern for international relations more than ever.

But before going further, what do we mean by empathy? As with other concepts we discuss, it is complicated and highly contested. An interdisciplinary survey of empathy for a volume on social neuroscience identified no less than eight distinct phenomena that researchers have treated as empathy, and concluded that there is really no clear basis for favoring one scheme over another, so all we can do is just be clear and consistent in our own work (Batson, 2009). Following that injunction, we note that one common understanding of empathy is the ability and/or experience of feeling what another feels. Recent brain science has provided evidence in the form of fMRI scans that people indeed do just that, as "watching another person experience pain, for example, engages the same emotion-related neural circuits that are engaged when one experiences pain oneself, and the brains of people who report having high levels of empathy toward others exhibit this effect more strongly" (Greene, 2013, pp. 37–38).

Psychologists have found several prominent triggers for empathy, one of the most reliable of which is its key evolutionary origins in *neotenous features*, or the geometry of a juvenile face. More colloquially known as '*cuteness*,' these characteristics include large head and eyes, small nose, jaw, body, and limbs, and are evoked not just by humans but other species (Pinker, 2011, p. 580). The familiar depiction of children for humanitarian appeals thus has a grounding in neuroscience, as does IR research which has found that this phenomenon has played key roles in some advocacy campaigns.

Another finding of psychologists is that empathy tends to be activated when encountering the sufferings of specific individuals, known as the *identifiable victim effect* (Cohen et al., 2015; Lee and Feeley, 2016). Thomas Schelling first discussed this effect in 1968 noting that "in almost all cases an individual life described in detail elicits more emotional reactions and aid than an equivalent life described as a statistic."[24] Politicians have long understood it, although it may be apocryphal that it was Stalin who said, "the death of one man is a tragedy; the death of a million is a statistic."

---

[24] Schelling (1968), as quoted by Lee and Feeley (2016).

Research has shown that "people are much more willing to aid identified individuals than unidentified or statistical victims" (Small et al., 2007). One experiment gave people the opportunity to contribute $5 of their earnings from participating in the experiment to the charity Save the Children. One group of respondents gave more than twice the amount to feed a seven-year-old African girl named Rokia, of whom they were shown a picture, than another group who were asked to donate to the same organization working to save millions of Africans (statistical lives) from hunger (Slovic et al., 2016). This provides a psychological explanation for the widespread practice among humanitarians of appealing to people through compelling personal stories, a tactic frequently found in the norms literature as helping propel the success of advocacy campaigns. This effect is powerfully elicited by the personalization of direct experience, but can also be elicited by imagery (Price, 1998). A recent example was the spike in global attention to Syrian refugees sparked by the photograph of Syrian child Aylan Kurdi washed up drowned on a Turkish island, which spurred greater donations to refugee assistance (Slovic et al., 2017). Such images provoke a direct emotional response: a process that can be activated not only by actual observation, but also by listening to stories, and visualizing or imagining various scenarios, though there may be differences in the evoked potentials for each modality (Watson and Greenberg, 2009, pp. 127–128). Importantly, "visual thinking is generally more emotionally evocative than verbal thinking" (Greene, 2014, p. 704). These factors have been sewn together in the development of this capacity for empathy: perceptual triggers originally developed to be responsive to signs of distress by one's own child can be activated by other children, baby animals, stuffed animals, cartoon characters, and even stories in newspapers about the suffering of far-away people (Graham et al., 2013, p. 12). Berenguer (2010) notes that the effect of empathy extends to improving environmental attitudes and behaviors. These phenomena have been frequently mentioned in the IR norms literature, providing added interdisciplinary robustness to a variety of experimental, discourse analysis, and field research methods (Crawford, 2002; Keck and Sikkink, 1998).

A third potential mechanism for altruism that has garnered tremendous recent attention has been the discovery of mirror neurons. First detected in primates by neuroscientists in 1992 who discovered that certain neurons in the brains of monkey's fired the same way when they watched a person pick up a raisin as when they picked up a raisin themselves, the idea that we may automatically experience other's experiences through such mirror neurons ignited a flurry of attention including as a source of empathy. Marcus Holmes has led the way in probing the implications of the kinds of effects attributed to these mirroring processes for IR, arguing that "face-to-face diplomacy is important to world politics because it is . . . an unrivaled mechanism for intention understanding," which represents "a relatively thin version of empathy" (Holmes, 2018, pp. 3, 20–21). The mirroring system, in particular, supports the hypothesis that the way we *understand* the intentions of others is by simulating their intentions in our own brains. Holmes points to this mirroring system, drawing from a variety of neuroscientists to arrive at the important position that "empathy is not causing the neurons to fire, but rather the neurons firing *constitutes* empathy" (Holmes, 2018, pp. 20–21).

At the same time, many psychologists also emphasize the limitations of empathy. Pinker ultimately concludes that empathy is inadequate to explain moral progress over the centuries:

> Empathy is a circle that may be stretched, but its elasticity is limited by kinship, friendship, similarity, and cuteness. It reaches a breaking point long before it encircles the full set of people that reason tells us should fall within our moral concern. It is reason that teaches us the tricks for expanding our empathy and how/when to parlay our compassion for strangers into action-able policy. (Pinker, 2011, p. 668)

Pinker's metaphor of a circle that needs to include the full set of people who should fall within our moral concern, is similar to one used by Helen Fein, a scholar of genocide, who speaks of "a realm of obligation." Fein argues that one of the explanations for genocide is a process through which individuals are excluded from the realm of obligation (Fein, 1993). Presumably, the inverse of excluding people from the realm of obligation is expanding the circle to include all people in a realm of obligation.

This helps square what could otherwise be a paradox in light of the way these issues have often been framed in IR – "states only care about themselves" say realists, while "we have shown people do care about even distant others" say constructivists. "But 'in-group bias' is pervasive," responded Jonathan Mercer, providing an early psychological critique of more sanguine constructivist accounts of the convergences of identity that can propel shared norms (Mercer, 1995, pp. 229–252). Psychology tells us both those stressing innate capacities for empathy and in-group bias are right, albeit each partially so: humans are wired for both altruism and tribalism, the issue really is how tight or expansive is the circle of those who come to count as part of "us." Even as the ways people understand empathy is embedded in political and cultural contexts, the "dynamic process of empathy always contains an immanent potential for transformation of the self and of self-other relationships" (Head, 2016, p. 104).

Several key issues bear unpacking here. First, what might it possibly mean to say people are "wired" in contradictory ways? Second, what accounts for the fact that we too often see the worst excesses of tribalism that discount the sufferings of others or indeed inflict it upon them, while at other times we see stunning actions of humanitarianism even for distant strangers? To address these central issues, first we address the limitations of empathy itself as a mobilizer of altruistic behavior, in terms of scale and by distinguishing it from sympathy and compassion.

### 3.6.1 Altruism: From Empathy to Sympathy and Compassion

One of the key issues is the scalability of empathy up from the identifiable victim effect mentioned previously. As Pinker notes, it is one thing for experiments to show we have a strong tendency to sympathize with others in need, but another to generalize one's sympathy to the group that the character represents. Similarly, Greene argues that most people exhibit only "parochial altruism" (Greene, 2013, pp. 39, 50, 54).

Importantly, some of the very same research confirming the identifiable victim effect has also found that not only do such personal anecdotes more powerfully elicit altruism than statistics, but in fact that as numbers of victims increase, empathy actually *decreases*, a tendency which may begin to kick in even when the number of victims goes from one to two! (Slovic et al., 2016, pp. 640–644). "Psychophysical numbing" is the phenomena of being overwhelmed by statistics of mass suffering. It thus produces "compassion fade," whereby increases in the number of victims decreases how much respondents care (Slovic et al., 2016, p. 642). Recent research (Faulkner, 2018) shows that encouraging people to empathize with distant individuals can foster cosmopolitan helping, but Faulkner only asks research subjects to take the point of view of one individual, and thus does not take into account such compassion fade.

While it is common to understand empathy as the source of altruism, some psychological research has stressed that empathy can impede altruistic behavior. Singer and Klimecki point out that an empathetic response to suffering can result in empathetic distress or compassion, both of which are empathetic responses but different emotions; empathetic distress is in fact "accompanied by the desire to withdraw from a situation in order to protect oneself from excessive negative feelings," whereas it is compassion that is properly thought of as the pro-social emotion (Singer and Klimecki, 2014). Research has shown the ways that empathy is "difficult and unpleasant – it wore people out. This is consistent with other findings suggesting that vicarious suffering not only leads to bad decision-making but also causes burnout and withdrawal" (Bloom, 2016). This is most important as it provides a neuro/psychological foundation to explain limitations of receptivity to moral entrepreneurship such as compassion fatigue. Practitioners of moral advocacy thus need to consider what kind of messaging may produce counterproductive numbing when it comes to behavior.

Other researchers help explain how empathy does sometimes elicit not just caring beliefs but pro-social behavior, though for many this is better captured with the term compassion. "Compassion is feeling *for* and not feeling *with* the other" (Singer and Klimecki, 2014, p. R875). This leads "to kinder behavior toward others. It has all the benefits of empathy and few of the costs" (Bloom, 2016). This distinction is similar to the one that other researchers make between empathy – feeling the other's emotional state – and sympathy – not *feeling* the same oneself but rather commiserating with another's unpleasant state, which some have argued is more likely to induce ameliorative action (Pinker, 2011, pp. 552, 584–590).

We do not believe that IR norms theory or practical advocacy has yet sufficiently caught up with these interesting distinctions in moral psychology between empathy and other emotions and reasoning that might form a more reliable basis for pro-social behavior.

## 4 Relevant IR Norms Research Incorporating Findings from Psychology and Neuroscience

### 4.1 Norms and the Dual Processing Brain

Historically, virtually all schools of thought within IR tended to ignore, take for granted, or marginalize the role of intuitions and emotions (Crawford, 2013; Jeffery, 2014). With the exception of important early work by Crawford, even most constructivists were not attentive to emotions in their discussions of norms (Crawford, 2013). Constructivist scholars have been aware of the role of emotions in transnational advocacy networks and moral entrepreneurship, but they often did not discuss it at length or theorize it.[25] Some constructivist norm theory gestured toward the literature on the dual processing brain but did not engage it deeply (Finnemore and Sikkink, 1998, p. 915). But the findings on the dual processing brain began to enter into international relations more generally (Kertzer and Tingley, 2018) and by now, such findings are at the forefront of the so-called new "behavioral revolution" in IR (Hafner-Burton et al., 2017).

Constructivists have tended to put more emphasis on the reasoning side of the dual processing brain than on emotions and moral intuitions, as demonstrated by the long line of research in IR discussing the role of moral persuasion, socialization, learning, and deliberation (Deitelhoff, 2009; Deitelhoff and

---

[25] For example, the word *emotions* is barely mentioned in Keck and Sikkink (1998).

Müller, 2005; Finnemore, 1996; Risse, 2000). In this work, constructivists drew on the preponderant tradition in political theory and philosophy more broadly that approached the topic of morality through deliberative reason, an approach which either implicitly or explicitly regarded emotion and intuitions as a basis for morality with suspicion.

The IR literature on processes of persuasion and pressure has not adequately come to grips with how moral intuitions and the myriad of cognitive biases could help us understand the uptake of advocacy campaign techniques, including attempts to foster change. Crawford (2002, 2009) addresses these issues in her research. Renee Jeffery draws on moral neuroscience to extensively and persuasively unpack the widespread contemporary view among moral psychologists that both emotions/intuitions and reasoning are essential to morality, and then relates these findings to understanding questions of global poverty (Jeffery, 2014). But Crawford and Jeffery are in a small minority of IR scholars applying brain science, and in particular the role of emotion to international ethics.

More recently, IR theorists are paying more attention to the intuitive side of the brain. Burcu Bayram, for example, uses psychological theories about social identity to explore decision makers' positions on compliance with international law (Bayram, 2017). In a study of German parliamentarians, she finds variation in the degree to which decision makers believe in the norm about the obligation to comply with international law. This variation is best explained by the social identity of the parliamentarians, in particular, a strong cosmopolitan social identity is the best explanation for support for the norm. In those decision makers, this strong identity in turn elicits the reflexive, rapid, and heuristic reasoning style characteristic of "system 1" intuitive processing (Bayram, 2017). This research shows promise of survey experiments of actual decision makers to test hypotheses about the dual processing brain.

## 4.2 Harm and Empathy

The findings from MFT have pointed to the importance of care/harm moral concern. Extensive research on the so-called Trolley problem helps makes our understandings of perceptions of harm more precise. These are psychological studies of the famous philosophy dilemmas of whether one should divert an out-of-control train coming down a track, an action that will directly kill one person but save several more. Results of these studies show that not only are people worried about harming others, but they are more worried about it if they themselves have to physically participate in the harm (Edmonds, 2014).

MFT has been used and tested by IR scholars, but mainly by those working on the impact of public opinion on US foreign policy, or those using data from US surveys (Kertzer et al., 2014; Kreps and Maxey, 2018; Rathbun and Stein, 2019, Smetana and Vranka 2020). There is also research by American politics scholars testing the impact of MFT primarily on US domestic policy debates (Clifford et al., 2015; Ryan, 2014). Bayram and Holmes (2020, p 822) find in their surveys "that affective empathy not only predicts individual variation in aid preferences but also explains why some individuals are less sensitive to aid effectiveness and more sensitive to recipient deservingness." There has been much less attention from norms researchers working on the implications of MFT for emergence, diffusion, and resonance of transnational norms.

Joshua Greene has given the difference between direct and indirect harm extended attention, and his results and theory provide a complex neurological explanation for these findings in the IR literature concerning these types of harms that are more likely than others to elicit opprobrium. David Traven in turn has skillfully applied these and related insights to norms of warfare, showing how they help us understand, from the neurological level, the prevalence of a norm against killing civilians that proscribes such action but only when it is intentional, not when it is a side effect. Informed by what he calls a naturalistic theory of moral cognition derived from cognitive science, social psychology, and social neuroscience, Traven argues that civilian protection rules have developed these distinctions because they "*fit* with cognitive-emotional biases ... [emphasis added]" and because of that, "should be more durable than other norms of war" (Traven, 2015, p. 569). Notions of "fit" or "resonance" or "match" have been prevalent in the IR norms literature, and Traven provides a plausible neuroscientific/psychological grounding that "sees the moral mind as a complex cognitive system that has intuitive-emotional biases and higher-order reasoning abilities," which can improve our analysis of international norms by seeing these norms not as "an outgrowth of cultural and discursive changes" but more accurately as "evolved moral psychology in a progressively changing contextual environment" (Traven, 2015, p. 582). Traven's is just the kind of application of neuroscientific and moral psychological research to international norms that points to an enriching research agenda going forward, even if his analysis does not resolve questions about variation and norm robustness, as he admittedly confines his claims to tendencies and not norm effectiveness (see Price, 2020).

Holmes (2018, p. 41, citing Mansbridge) makes the significant leap for IR to argue that "[face-to-face contact] seems to increase the actual congruence of interests by encouraging the empathy by which individual members make out one another's interests their own." Others vigorously dispute these claims, as

Holmes openly concedes (Holmes, 2018, pp. 41, 63–67). Pinker, for one, is far less sanguine, concluding that empathy is not an automatic reflection of mirror neurons, but can be turned on and off (Pinker, 2011, pp. 577–578). Does identification with another have to come first to kick in empathy, or can stimuli like face-to-face interactions among rivals or even enemies stimulate that empathy in the first place? We echo the call from neuroscientists noted by Holmes for interdisciplinary debate and comparing methods and evidence on these matters as an exciting research agenda some moral psychologists are currently pursuing.

In another application focused on diplomatic negotiations, Holmes and Yarhi-Milo note that both empathy and beliefs about a counterpart's ability to empathize, "are critical to the process and outcomes of diplomatic negotiations" (Holmes and Yarhi-Milo, 2017). It is interesting to note that they define the term empathy as *understanding* other's feelings, rather than *feeling* them emotionally as is the more common definition of empathy, showing the variety of conceptualizations among those working with empathy.

Crawford has likewise argued that "The potential role of empathy in world politics is deep and wide," and that diplomacy, trade, communication, and cultural interaction are all opportunities to develop interpersonal and intergroup empathy (Crawford, 2014, p. 550). In an original theoretical contribution, Crawford argues that empathy can be *institutionalized*, in organizations like the European Union and other pluralistic security communities, and in doctrines like responsibility to protect. But emotions like fear can also be institutionalized, as they have been in the United States since 9/11, in color-coded terrorist threat-level policies, physical structures, like fences, or technologies like X-rays at airports, as well as military doctrines of preemption and preventative war (Crawford, 2014, pp. 549–550). Crawford's concepts of the institutionalization of emotions like empathy, including in international institutions and doctrines, is a contribution by an international relations theorist that should be of interest to moral psychology. The argument we make in this volume is related to Crawford's argument about the institutionalization of emotions. We claim that transnational norms begin as moral intuitions, but through a process of reasoning (alongside power and bargaining), in which emotion plays a role but does not predominate, these norms are later institutionalized in international law and institutions.

## 4.3 Context, Culture, and Cognition

Excessive attention to moral intuitions ought not lead us to disregard the political processes and contexts within which norm debates occur.

Psychological research embraces that culture changes the brain. In a statement that puts the "social" back in construction in this analysis that has focused on micro and neurofoundations, Joseph Heath has noted that, "Perhaps the most disconcerting finding of 20th century social science was that most of what we like to think of as 'morality' is actually not in our heads, but depends upon environmental scaffolding as well" (Heath, 2014, p. 102) – that is, the contextual psychological triggers and social cues that have been shown to have a tremendous impact on our moral choices. For example, we have long known from both psychological and political studies about the ways in which humans seek conformity with their social context, in both profound and mundane ways (Asch, 1951). As an example of profound ways, this is related to what Hannah Arendt meant when she said that Adolf Eichmann exemplified the "banality of evil." He was not a monster, she argued, but a man who could not tell right from wrong, and thus had a conscience that spoke with the voice of civilized society around him. The voice of civilized society in Nazi Germany embraced the Final Solution, and thus so did Eichmann (Arendt, 2006).

Following up on Arendt, the "situational psychology" of scholars like Milgram stressed how situational forces and group dynamics matter more for moral outcomes than the predispositions of the actual participants. These scholars highlight how relatively small interventions in the situation in experiments can alter the norm context and the outcomes. For example, Milgram's experiment (1963) is best remembered for showing how far individuals will obey when told by an authority to give electric shocks to subjects. In this sense, it confirms the impact of the moral foundation of obedience to authority. Less well remembered are the various ways in which the manipulation of the context changed the outcome. So, for example, Milgram found that adding two other participants (confederates) who refused to obey the orders to give shocks reduced the level of obedience of the group from 65 per cent to 10 per cent (Milgram, 2009).

In terms of mundane ways that context shapes behavior, in experiments on conformity in the 1950s asking participants to compare lengths of a line, Asch found that participants regularly chose the wrong answer if that was what the majority chose. But the presence of just one confederate who went against the majority choice reduced conformity by as much as 80 per cent. Research also suggests that scientific training can help individuals resist contextual pressures toward conformity. Perrin and Spencer (1980) for example, replicated the original Asch experiment using engineering, mathematics, and chemistry students as subjects, and found dramatically lower levels of conformity to erroneous group estimates.

These findings about the importance of breaking conformity and the conditions under which it can happen have important implications for norm campaigns and courageous resistance (Thalhammer, 2007). For example, as in the case with the STEM students, some kinds of training can make individuals less likely to cave into conformity to erroneous groups beliefs. In the case of both Milgram and Ash, we see that the voice of just one or two resisters who go against the majority choice can reduce conformity dramatically. We might think of norm entrepreneurs as playing this role in norms campaigns, giving other bystanders space to reduce their conformity to old norms and embrace new ones.

Psychologists describe how situational factors, especially perceptions of peer behavior, have been shown to be far more important than personality differences in explaining moral choices. In experiments, people can be induced to cheat or bribe or refrain from cheating or bribing by making slight adjustments to the information given to them about the number of others engaging in said behavior. "Thus, morality is best thought of not as something that lies within our hearts or our heads, but as a complex cultural artifact, that gets reproduced and modified over time, and that 'lives' primarily in the interactions between individuals" (Heath, 2014, p. 106).

Thus, while the Section 4.2 focused on (sub)agent-level dynamics, these findings validate the importance constructivists place on structural factors of culture and norms, and the ways in which different local and international contexts may lead to different norms outcomes. As Wexler notes in his presentation of an extensive array of neurobiological, psychobiological, and psychological research data on the relationship between the biological and the social, the neuropsychological "internal structures of each generation of young adults differ from those of their parents" (Wexler, 2006, p. 6).

But as individuals in our societies increasingly self-select into like-minded social and professional groups, opportunities for resistance to alter group conformity may be reduced. IR scholars have often noted that a propitious condition for change is a sense of perceived crisis; this would suggest that significant, rapid change is not the norm but generally the exception, yet still possible. This dovetails nicely with psychological perspectives that adults are capable of making changes in their internal worlds to adjust to major changes in their external worlds, and many of these stressful adjustments eventually prove successful. These adaptations, however, generally are more difficult the older the individual; are experienced as unpleasant; can have negative physical and emotional consequences; are not always successful; and, as a result, are avoided when possible (Wexler, 2006, p. 171).

As Mercer notes:

culture shapes cognition (Henrich et al. 2010) . Cultural neuroscientists find
that "both the structure and the function of the developing human brain is
shaped both by the environment and by cultural experiences" (Chia and
Ambady 2007, 238). Culture changes the brain's architecture. For example,
divergent philosophical traditions lead to differences in neural activity (Chia
and Ambady 2007). Culture influences feeling and thinking, which provides
one explanation for why feeling like a group is common. (Mercer, 2014,
p. 523)

But most importantly, we need to understand how moral intuitions and
emotions interact with situational factors. For example, Price took on genetic
explanations for the chemical weapons (CW) taboo which speculated that this
norm derived from a genetic human predisposition to be fearful of poison like
spiders and snakes. This was ruled out insofar as Price's research found that
many soldiers exposed to CW in World War I just did not have that kind of
reaction, and some even championed CW as the weapon of the future. Yet moral
psychology perspectives might help unpack this relationship a bit more subtly to
allow that some such influences may have played a part for some people, even as
they cannot be sufficient in and of themselves. Consider a classic study by
Mineka and Cook cited by Graham et al. (2013):

Young rhesus monkeys, who showed no prior fear of snakes – including
plastic snakes – watched a video of an adult monkey reacting fearfully (or
not) to a plastic snake (or to plastic flowers). The monkeys learned from
a single exposure to a snake-fearing monkey to be afraid of the plastic snake,
but a single exposure to a flower-fearing monkey did nothing. This is an
example of "preparedness" (Seligman, 1971). Evolution created something
"organized in advance of experience" that made it easy for monkeys – and
humans (DeLoache & LoBue, 2009) – to learn to fear snakes. Evolution did
not simply install a general-purpose learning mechanism which made the
monkeys take on all the fears of adult role models equally. (Graham et al.,
2013, p. 8)

That points to but one possible mechanism of the transference of intuitive fears
as a potential source of norms. Greene's account nicely summarizes the range of
mechanisms of the intuitive sources of morality:

Automatic settings can function well only when they have been shaped by
trial-and-error experience. This may be the experience of our biological
ancestors, as reflected in, for example, a genetic predisposition to fear snakes.
Our automatic settings may be shaped by the experience of our cultural
"ancestors," as reflected in a fear of guns, despite one's having never been
harmed by one. Finally, our automatic settings are shaped by our own trial
and error, as when one learns to fear hot stoves by touching them. These three
mechanisms – genetic transmission, cultural transmission, and learning from

personal experience – are the only mechanisms known to endow human automatic cognitive processes with the information they need to function well. For one of our automatic settings to function well, its design must be informed by someone's trial-and-error experience. (Greene, 2014, p. 714)

This provides neurological connective tissue to help us understand how cultural dispositions can become intuitive and vice versa. In the case of the chemical weapons (CW) taboo, Price (1997) postulated that a key for its development over the last century or so has been something of an "anachronistic fear" issuing from the fact that CW have not been used often, and thus been "gotten used to" as another unavoidable tragedy of conflict. These moral psychology findings dovetail nicely with this account and provide a microfoundation for this global norm.

Such mechanisms can provide a neurofoundation connecting constellations of different types of politics at the domestic and transnational levels. For instance, it surely is no accident that the period in the 1990s that witnessed perhaps the height of liberal internationalism through the institutionalization of a variety of liberal norms – including the International Criminal Court (ICC), Chemical Weapons Convention, Landmines Convention, World Trade Organization, Comprehensive Test Ban Treaty[26] – was propelled by like-minded coalitions led by governments and their activist leaders like Nelson Mandela and foreign ministers such as Gareth Evans, Robin Cook, and Lloyd Axworthy, among others. Such projects are falling on hard times with the ascendancy of a variety of right-wing and authoritarian governments, including not just backlash but backtracking on institutionalized commitments as with some governments pulling out of the ICC.

## 5 Prescriptions for Research: Toward a New Research Agenda

In this section, we highlight prescriptions for research using brain science findings that may provide explanations at the neurological and psychological levels for key debates in the IR norms literature and help unpack and provide more nuance to other claims in the IR literature. We are particularly interested in applying findings from research on the dual processing brain and from MFT to research on norm emergence and norm success or failure. The first, and most obvious recommendation for this research agenda is that constructivist norms researchers need to be more open-minded and persistent about studying the neuroscience and psychology literature as possible sources of relevant hypotheses for future norms research. Some of our more psychologically inclined IR colleagues may choose to go the route of collaborating with neuroscientists to

---

[26] This last not yet into force, but largely abided by as a norm.

do jointly designed fMRI research and other forms of coauthored research. There will otherwise continue to be a "division of labor" between psychologists and IR norm theorists, of course, but a division of labor only exists where there is a genuine dialogue and engagement which we encourage and hope to achieve here. And we believe the division of labor should be a two-way street where theoretical and empirical contributions can be made on both sides.

We think that IR norms scholars could benefit from testing some of the hypotheses generated in moral psychology using traditional political-science methods of qualitative case studies as well as quantitative analysis and survey experiments of norm setters in diverse international settings. The many findings from close empirical case studies and larger N studies of international norms by IR scholars have much to contribute by way of validating or challenging the conclusions drawn from laboratory research, recognizing, of course, that sometimes scholars from across these fields draw upon similar methods such as surveys and survey experiments. Some methods that have been so important for IR constructivist research but are less familiar to neuroscience and moral psychology, including qualitative case studies, discourse analysis, and process tracing, will continue to yield findings that will be essential to the overall project we advocate here.[27]

While studies of US foreign policy and foreign policy more generally using psychological literatures are important and useful, less has been done to use psychological research to advance the agenda on the particular questions that animate research on the origins of transnational norms and why some win out over others. The research agenda we propose here – mostly by way of forwarding hypotheses for future research – distinguishes how we expect norm theory to relate to the foreign policy of individual states from how it relates to the transnational resonance and institutionalization of norms.

## 5.1 Incorporating Insights from Moral Foundation Theory and the Dual Processing Brain

In Section 4, we identified an imbalance in the IR norms literature that still continues to place more emphasis on the rational processes of persuasion, argument, and deliberation as explanations for norm acceptance. To correct this imbalance, one central research recommendation for understanding the microfoundations of norm emergence, resonance, and effectiveness is that IR researchers make more concerted attempts to explore the intuitive side of the dual processing brain, and in particular the links between the moral foundations proposed by MFT and norm theory, with suitable modifications as the validity of

---

[27] For an in-depth discussion, including best practices, see Bennett and Checkel (2014).

MFT itself continues to be tested. Psychologists have started to do this work (Stolerman and Lagnado, 2018), as have scholars working on foreign policy of specific states, but it is much less common among norms theorists of transnational norms. This path may help theorists deal with some of the debates and conundrums of norm theory and advance in these areas where we seem stuck, such as the two key norm research questions we highlighted in the first paragraphs of this Element – why do norms emerge and why do some norms win out over others? Promising hypotheses come from the literature discussed above about moral intuitions in the dual process brain.

Norms researchers have developed crucial mid-level theory about why some norms emerge and advance and others do not. The main explanations put forward stress norm entrepreneurs, compatibility with interests, and role of policy gatekeepers, diffusion, resonance, and cultural match between a global norm and a target country, or – because new norms can be "grafted" onto existing ones through strategic framing or through processes of localization – existing norms can be adapted to different cultural settings (Acharya, 2004; Checkel, 1999; Crawford, 2002; Klotz, 1995; Nadelmann, 1990). A central characteristic of virtually all theories of norms is that processes of norm acceptance and norm internalization rely primarily on mechanisms of social sanctions and pressures rather than on legal punishment. Such social sanctions usually include some forms of shaming and ostracism. This was recognized as a key mechanism of the norm life cycle (Finnemore and Sikkink, 1998), and has more recently been referred to as rhetorical coercion by some authors (Krebs and Jackson, 2016). It is also consistent with the mechanisms identified by some psychological researchers, including DIT approaches discussed previously. We do not reject this mid-level theory, including our own past research, as we promote this new research agenda. We only suggest that it has not been sufficient ultimately to explain why some norms emerge and other do not.

Many of these explanations stressed the importance of some kind of match between existing structures and the norm proposals put forward by agents. For example, Price showed how some advocates for a new norm prohibiting antipersonnel landmines in the 1990s connected that norm with other prohibitions on weapons deemed indiscriminate like CW, and that the CW taboo itself was the product of numerous grafts that resulted in significant changes in the scope of the norm (Price, 1998). These arguments are useful and persuasive, but they still do not satisfactorily address the bigger question of why some earlier norms lend themselves to grafting or localization in the first place. These arguments are essentially path-dependent explanations: that is, once a particular "norm path" begins, a new norm is more likely to advance when it connects to an older norms path or resonates with existing domestic culture.

We suggest that some of what has been seen as "grafting" or resonating with previously entrenched norms could also be viewed as the result of similar successful appeals to commonplace moral intuitions, for example, about fairness or harm. Neuroscience can provide a micro-foundation for norm receptivity at the individual level for this phenomenon. This is exhibited in an experiment related by neuroscientist Daniel Levitin, showing how humans have associational neural networks which activate related ideas due to spreading activation in a similar part of the brain (Levitin, 2014, pp. 53–55). When asked to remember a list of words like rest, tired, dream, snore, bed, etc., 60 percent of people will identify the word "sleep" even though it is not in the list.

We hypothesize that this neurological network explanation may be useful to explain some of the grafting, resonance, and match phenomena often observed by IR scholars as important for transnational networks. New norms which are associated with existing accepted ideas may produce less psychic dissonance of radical change, and thus less intuitive resistance, that could subsequently drive easier ethical consideration and uptake. Further refinement of this idea could involve advocacy organizations testing which framing of norms in different cultural settings, and with different constituencies within those settings (such as conservative and liberal subjects) resonate with related accepted ideas and norms they could be packaged with. Such research could provide critical links between neurofoundations and processes of localization and transnationalization.

## 5.2 Explanations for the Emergence and Resonance of Norms

It continues to be a paradox that scholars should grant so little significance to the nature or content of ideas as one possible explanation for transnational norm emergence or resonance. Simply put, norms scholars have virtually never made an argument that any particular ideas are intrinsically more appealing than others. John Ruggie has referred to "captivating social metaphors" in some of his work, but has not clarified why a particular idea or norm might be more captivating than others (Ruggie, 1982, p. 386). Finnemore and Sikkink briefly reviewed arguments about the content or nature of norms, citing work by Keck and Sikkink arguing that the "intrinsic characteristics" of certain issues could help to explain why transnational advocacy networks were more likely to be successful on some issues (especially those involving bodily harm of vulnerable populations, and equality of opportunity) than on others (Finnemore and Sikkink, 1998; Keck and Sikkink, 1998, pp. 26–28). But these hypotheses were never properly developed further or tested by the authors or by other authors, to our awareness.

We argue that the moral intuitions provide some of the microfoundations for helping explain transnational norm emergence and resonance. In order to do so, however, we must call into question the blank-slate model of cognition that McDermott and Lopez have called one of the characteristics of constructivism and most other social science research (McDermott and Lopez, 2012; Pinker, 2002). Most constructivist norm theory implicitly embraces the blank-slate model and implies we can make a norm out of most anything. While useful in the early stages of norms research to contest the materialism of most approaches to IR, it created problems of empirical indeterminacy and ethical relativism.[28] We believe that the preponderance of evidence in the literature discussed in the first half of this Element makes it impossible to sustain the blank-slate model of cognition, nor does constructivism per se require it. Given the dual process brain's capacity for reasoning, neuroplasticity, and the sensitivity of the brain to its environment, there is still ample room for social construction, without also insisting on the brain as a blank slate.

For example, some empirical research has shown that people who strongly hold the moral foundations of care and fairness (defined as equality) are more likely to support human rights (Stolerman and Lagnado, 2018). But giving up the blank-slate model of cognition does not mean automatically accepting some arguments made by psychologists. For example, Greene has argued that human rights arguments are predominately related to the intuitive brain, *not* to the manual mode of deliberation – an argument for which we present disconfirming evidence later in this Element and that others like Pinker support, citing the importance of reason.

Sometimes IR also needs to translate and link literatures in IR and psychology that have been struggling with similar issues using different language. For example, using MFT we could say that Keck and Sikkink's arguments about the success of transnational campaigns around bodily harm to vulnerable or innocent victims and equality of opportunity can be understood as an implicit hypothesis that those campaigns were successful because those arguments appealed to universal moral intuitions, in particular to care/harm, and fairness. This would allow us to reformulate the Keck and Sikkink hypothesis in such a way as to make it more generalizable and to expand its explanatory power. Using both MFT and the literature on trolleyology could provide microfoundations for the existing but as yet underdeveloped and untested hypotheses that issues involving harm and a short causal link between the perpetrator and the victim will be more amenable to transnational norms campaigns.

---

[28] We thank an anonymous reviewer for this formulation.

Moral foundations theorists originally conceived of fairness as including mainly concerns about rights, justice, and equality, which are more strongly endorsed by political liberals. They reformulated the theory in 2011, however, based on new data, and began also to emphasize what they called proportionality, by which they mean the belief that people should be rewarded in proportion to what they contribute, even if that guarantees unequal outcomes. Their surveys showed that proportionality is often supported by everyone, but is more strongly endorsed by conservatives.[29] We suggest for future research that the idea of equality of opportunity is a bridge between equality and proportionality and thus is more likely to receive more support from both liberals and conservatives than equality of outcomes. A second reformulated Keck and Sikkink hypothesis to research would emphasize resonance with the moral foundation of fairness, but, by stressing equality of opportunity, it also references the more conservative sense of fairness that includes proportionality rather than equality of outcomes.

Similar arguments could be made for the research findings of Klotz on apartheid, which involved both bodily harm and fairness, Crawford's conclusions on decolonization, involving fairness, and Price's arguments on chemical weapons and landmines, involving bodily harm (Crawford, 2002; Klotz, 1995; Price, 1997, 1998). But this hypothesis about the appeal to moral intuitions only gets us so far, and does not explain, for example, why there was more success with banning antipersonnel landmines, but not small arms, both which involve bodily harm. Here, it may be useful to draw on the other moral foundations to explain push-back on some issues but not others. At least in the United States, the ownership of small arms is closely connected to the liberty moral foundation, where the ownership of landmines does not invoke such a connection. Here political sources of morality are critically needed alongside neuro/psychological moral foundations.

The moral foundations literature may also help IR researchers move ahead thinking about those campaigns and issues where different moral foundations come most powerfully into conflict with one another. To return to one of the puzzles we posed in the Introduction to this Element about the rapid spread of norms in favor of LGBTQ rights, we would argue that global LGBTQ campaigns are more likely to succeed than fail, because their issue content demanding equality of opportunity for LGBTQ individuals (in work, marriage, etc.), will resonate with moral intuitions of both liberals and some conservatives. In this sense, we would expect these campaigns to resemble other successful global campaigns for equality of opportunity, like the antislavery movement,

---

[29] https://moralfoundations.org/.

the women's suffrage movement, and the anti-apartheid movement. At the same time, campaigns for LGBTQ rights come into direct conflict with other powerful moral intuitions around "sanctity/purity" around the world that have long demonized homosexuality as deviant and impure, as well as the moral foundation about obedience to authority, in this case religious authority. One hypothesis that follows is that such traditional authorities like churches may be particularly influential catalysts of change should they shift their positions on such issues. Might Catholics thus fall in line with recent statements by the Pope that same sex couples should be covered by civil unions laws?

So moral foundations theory helps us understand why some norms that are connected to powerful moral foundations emerge in the first place, but not how to gauge which norms will succeed when two or more different moral foundations come into conflict with one another. This is an area that involves how moral foundations meet politics, and where IR norms researchers could make a contribution to the broader interdisciplinary debate.

### 5.2.1 Good Norms vs. Bad Norms?

Incorporating insights from MFT into norm theory may also be useful to address some increasingly unproductive debates among norm theorists, such as the debates over transnational advocacy around "good norms" and "bad norms." Some authors critique norms researchers for only studying progressive norms and "left-wing" movements such as those on human rights or the environment, but not conservative norms and right-wing advocacy on issues such as abortion, the right to bear guns, or anti-LGBTQ rights (Bob, 2013). The very definition of a norm is a standard of appropriate behavior – so people advocating norms themselves believe, almost by definition, that such norms are appropriate (i.e., "good"). But what the critique suggests is that too many norms researchers, who are often liberal, may be prone to study norms campaigns with which they agree, not norms campaigns with which they disagree.

MFT is useful in this regard, allowing us to move beyond simplistic distinctions such as good norms versus bad norms, or left-wing versus right-wing norms, and begin a more fine-grained categorization of the diverse kinds of moral considerations at stake in particular issues. We advocate including the full range of moral intuitions in thinking about and categorizing norms – including the liberty/oppression foundation – and also being attentive to different interpretations of a single foundation, such as the differences between the equality versus proportionality understandings of fairness. We would expect the full range of moral foundations to be useful to help explain the emergence and growth of norms movements, whether of the right or the left.

For example, the MFT approach can help us understand the rise of the kinds of rightwing norm campaigns that Clifford Bob has discussed in his work, such as transnational gun rights and anti-LGBTQ campaigns (Bob, 2012). MFT also gives more insights into anti-immigrant movements in many countries around the world, as based in the foundation of loyalty, and their emphasis on in-groups and out-groups. Antiabortion groups are an example of Haidt's point that conservatives also may care about issues of bodily harm, while at the same time also emphasizing the binding foundations of sanctity and obedience to authority, in this case, religious authority. The foundation involving obedience to authority is prominent in some norms campaigns such as the "pro-family" norms movement, or traditional values movements which are very much a reflection of the conservative moral intuitions about obedience to traditional authority, including the father in the family; the Iman, rabbi, priest, or preacher in the mosque, synagogue, or church; and the leaders in the country. This raises interesting research-agenda issues on the relative traction of religious versus secular norms, both in terms of longer-term trajectories, and in specific conflicts in a given norm debate.

A rough survey of the IR literature on norms and transnational advocacy reveals that more attention has indeed been devoted to liberal or leftwing transnational norms campaigns.[30] There are various possible reasons for this. One possibility is that there are actually more liberal or left-wing transnational advocacy campaigns. Another is that these campaigns were more unexpected by predominant realist and rationalist IR theories at the time and thus generated more scholarly attention than campaigns on more expected issues such as loyalty to nation or clan, obedience to authority, or outcomes that conformed with expectations of power and interests. It may also have been because right-wing transnational organizing by civil society groups arose later in reaction to the successes of previous progressive organizing. As long as abortion and same-sex relations, for example, were prohibited by both norms and laws in most parts of the world, there was no need for campaigns against them. It was with the advent of liberalized abortion laws, and the quite recent advances in LGBTQ rights that we understandably see the rise of countermovements. But these countermovements are not only against what is actually happening in the country at hand, but can be "anticipatory" countermovements, watching what

---

[30] The rough survey involved a keyword search on international norms, and transnational advocacy (separately) in the Harvard Library, and a categorization of the works. Approximately 75% of books and articles listed involved liberal or leftwing transnational campaigns (categorizing democracy and election monitoring as liberal) while the remaining 25% involved either those that were right wing or neither right wing nor left wing (general theory) or difficult to categorize (maternal and newborn survival, organ trafficking, diversity of cultural expressions, etc.).

is happening in other parts of the world, and taking action to prevent advances, for example, in LGBTQ rights (Weiss, 2013). All of these hypotheses could be investigated in future research to try to assess the exogenous and endogenous sources of transnational normative change including the interplay of the micro-foundations we are examining here.

Using MFT to more carefully categorize the diverse kinds of moral considerations at stake in different campaigns, norms theorists may be able to answer some of the questions in the previous paragraph. Also, MFT provides more nuanced and less loaded terms to categorize norms, compared to good or bad or right wing or left wing. When we tried to code the existing norms literature on the left-wing/right-wing continuum, if was difficult to categorize some issues, like sex trafficking or organ trafficking, maternal and newborn survival, or transnational crime, although all could be considered within the MFT category of harm/care, for example.

### 5.2.2 Which Norm Campaigns Will Succeed, and Which Will not?

IR norms literature is interested not only in why norms emerge and resonate, but also in which norm campaigns succeed in terms of getting their norms institutionalized in international treaties and multilateral organizations. What can we say about what norms are more likely to be institutionalized?

As Bob argues, some transnational networks based on conservative moral foundations have succeeded in producing backlash against existing norms and state policy, upsetting and "unsetting" agendas, and "unframing" or "hijacking" frames of their opponents. But notice all the negative concepts Bob is coining here: "unsetting," "unframing," "framejacking."[31] In the end, these groups have been better at sustaining existing traditional norms, and at blocking the proposals of others, than in moving forward their own global agendas. Right-wing transnational networks have been successful in leading to domestic policy change within many countries, but have not been as successful in drafting new international treaties, or embedding their norms in multilateral institutions. Instead, they often try to draft soft-law declarations and make appeals to customary law based on ambiguous state practice (Bob, 2012, p. 31). Why is this the case? MFT does not give us the elements to explain it. MFT helps us understand that these are often moral movements guided by moral intuitions, but not why these movements, guided by the binding moral intuitions, have not succeeded in institutionalizing their demands in new international norms or law.

---

[31] By framejacking, Bob refers, for example, to right-wing groups using rights or body integrity frames to contest other human rights movements (Bob, 2012, pp. 26–29.)

If we shift the lens to see that the "binding" intuitions are more likely to be about parochial moralities, and the "individualizing" ones are really about more expansive universalist (internationalist or cosmopolitan) moralities, we understand why the former are less likely candidates for transnational cooperation other than more instrumental tactical alliances. If it were moral intuitions only driving these successful campaigns, and if all moral intuitions were equally influential, we would expect to see treaties on all the moral intuitions, but we do not. As Greene has underscored in the US case, "social conservatives are not best described as people who place special value on authority, sanctity, and loyalty [they aren't loyal to UN authority, e.g.], but rather as tribal loyalists – loyal to their own authorities, their own religion, and themselves. This doesn't make them evil, but it does make them *parochial*" (Greene, 2013, p. 340). These insights are rich for understanding the underpinnings of normative IR debates between communitarianism and cosmopolitanism.

State actors with these parochial interests are more likely to try to attack and dismantle international norms and institutions they oppose. For example, as Bob argues, there is a "Baptist-Burqa" transnational advocacy network pushing back against LGBTQ rights around the world. These groups, however, are not promoting new norms as much as trying to preserve or strengthen existing norms. In the case of the anti-LGBTQ network, these efforts to preserve existing norms may involve what Weiss has called, "anticipatory homophobia," where the movement "responded far more to developments in the United States and elsewhere than to the overt expression of non-heteronormative identities or rights claims in the local community" (Weiss, 2013, p. 151).

But the network is more than just Baptists and Muslims, as it has found an important champion in Putin as well, with the support of the Russian Orthodox Church. In some cases, those with parochial values do try to extend their agenda globally. Russia has launched an international campaign for "traditional values," in the UN Human Rights Council, one of underlying purposes of which was to confront the liberal campaigns for LGBTQ rights, which Russia labels as deviant. In this campaign, Russia not only has the support of the Russian Orthodox Church, but also of other multinational religious right organizations (Hooper, 2016). For the Russian Orthodox church, the traditional values campaign was about factors that "divert human beings from the path of salvation," especially gender equality and LGBTQ rights (Horsfjord, 2016). In the language of MFT, these are campaigns about sanctity and traditional authority.

Despite the Baptist-Burqa-Orthodox alliance, 123 UN member states, including China and India, do not criminalize consensual same-sex sexual acts. Many of these states explicitly decriminalized, including twenty-four countries since 2000, while others never had a criminalizing provision in their Penal Codes

(Mendos, 2019). Since 2001, when the first country in the world, the Netherlands, allowed same-sex couples to marry, forty-two countries now permit same-sex marriage or make civil unions or registered partnerships available for same-sex couples.[32] The Baptist-Burqa network without doubt has engaged in anticipatory homophobia, and it may have blocked efforts to have LGBTQ rights embedded in positive international law, but it would take more research to ascertain this. While human rights law is definitive that no discrimination is permitted with regard to any status, there is no positive international law explicitly protecting the rights of people not to be discriminated against based on sexual orientation. The Yogyakarta Principles of 2006 are a declaration, not by states, but by a group of international human rights experts to outline a set of international principles of how existing human rights law should be interpreted with regard to sexual orientation and identity (International Commission of Jurists (ICJ), 2007).

If we look at the important literature on norm contestation, it is clear that contestation continues during much of the norm life cycle, and even norms that were considered well past a tipping point and with prescriptive status can and have been seriously challenged, if not yet reversed, as in the case of torture (Deitelhoff and Zimmermann, 2018, 2019; Kenkel and Cunliffe, 2016; Wiener, 2014). As damaging as these attacks on well-established norms have been, they have not deeply undermined the robustness of many international norms, nor yet resulted in the construction of new global norms, much less law. In their project on norm contestation, Zimmerman and Deitelhoff determined that the norms analyzed were not easily eroded, and that "despite direct challenges, they remained surprisingly robust": they concluded that "norm robustness is not determined by the relative power of norm challengers," but also other types of factors, including being embedded in institutions and law (Deitelhoff and Zimmermann, 2019, p. 2). They do not address, however, whether the intrinsic character of some norms led both to their incorporation in law and institutions in the first place and also made them more resilient to contestation. For example, with regard to the norm against torture, conservative actors found it difficult to contest the validity of the norm itself, so they tried to disguise their contestation of the anti-torture norm by engaging in covert arguments (Schmidt and Sikkink, 2019). Future research could attempt to validate if such dynamics hold across other issues.

One of the more powerful global countermovements, the transnational anti-bortion movement, has blocked and slowed the pace of liberalized abortion law, and in some countries has contributed to strict and even draconian enforcement of existing antiabortion laws. But over the past several decades, nearly fifty

---

[32] http://internap.hrw.org/features/features/marriage_equality/.

countries liberalized their abortion laws, sometimes incrementally, enabling legal abortion only for rape or when there is a threat to the mother's life, but in other cases in a truly transformative manner in favor of reproductive rights (Stensvold, 2016).[33] How microfoundational morals against harm interact with those about liberty and other moral foundations could provide telling insights about likely global trajectories.

### 5.2.3 Norms and Justifications

The research we have reviewed here puts the issue of how to treat justifications for policy in IR in a most interesting light. It is a long tradition in IR, and political thought more generally, to regard the moral justifications offered by politicians for policy as typically just masks for policies taken for other reasons, usually ones revolving around power and/or economic interests. Haidt and his colleagues would seem to largely agree in one sense, albeit for quite different reasons. It is not so much that what passes as moral discourse is in fact instrumental rationalization of decisions taken for the kinds of reasons often articulated by realists – namely deliberate, cold-hearted power calculations. If moral psychologists like Haidt are right, the rationalizations are more apt to be justifications for intuitive and often not self-conscious moral positions, a fundamental challenge to skeptical and rationalist accounts of political decision-making. So if intuitionists are right, morality matters *more* in that sense than would typically be conceded by a moral skeptic, though *moral reasoning* as such might figure *less* than many advocates of the role of morality in IR might suppose.

How have IR scholars thought of this? Justifications have long figured prominently in debates in IR about the role of ethics – from Hedley Bull's argument that justifications place some minimum boundaries upon political action since one cannot argue just anything and retain legitimacy that is important for order, to Kratochwil and Ruggie's insistence that a key to understanding the role of norms lies in studying the pattern of justifications for violations and reactions to them (Bull, 1977; Kratochwil and Ruggie, 1986). The latter injunction has proven to be a rich vein of evidence for scholars to show the development of norms over time, tracing how justifications for practices have changed such that what was once contested became no longer or much less so, an important metric for gauging the robustness of international norms.[34] To the extent moral psychologists are right, the justifications offered by politicians might reflect more genuine moral positions, albeit ones not

---

[33] Center for Reproductive Rights, "The World's Abortion Laws," https://reproductiverights.org /worldabortionlaws.

[34] See, among others, Crawford (2002); Finnemore (2003); Mueller (1996); Price (1997).

always rationally driven. Such a move would entail making a leap from surveys or fMRIs of individuals considering their own moral beliefs, to the deliberations and stratagems – and ultimately behavior – of political actors who have many other considerations to take into account that are not confronted by random citizens engaged in experiments. It is into precisely this gap that we think research of international politics often needs to be inserted, as we consider the stretch between explaining moral *beliefs* of citizens derived from experiments and the drivers of *behavior* of political actors.

## 5.3 What Contributions Can IR Research on Norms Make to Moral Psychology?

This engagement with psychology is not a one-way street. Political scientists could connect some of our insights about how norms and morality work in international relations to ongoing work in the brain sciences fields to bring research from the lab and field closer together. IR theory and empirical findings can add some important insights to these studies.

Leading moral psychologists have underscored the differences in how liberals and conservatives are morally wired. IR scholars have likewise shown that ordinary people carry IR paradigms around in their heads, and that we can speak of "folk realists," and "folk idealists." These beliefs are not the result of information, but are linked to other politically relevant orientations, especially being conservative or liberal (Kertzer and Mcgraw, 2012).

This could leave one with a more pessimistic outlook on moral convergence. But while we do not expect increasing convergence among citizens in a particular country as such, IR scholars have nonetheless documented the wider extension and acceptance of many liberal norms advanced across the globe, and institutionalized in international law and institutions, some of which in turn have provoked a notable backlash in recent years. These include efforts, among others, to restrain the conduct of war and protect civilians, including from rape, as well as efforts to curtail wars of aggression and limit the kinds of weapons that could be used in war, from dumdum bullets to landmines to chemical weapons; and efforts to protect workers' rights, provide equality for women, and create the entire human rights regime covering everything from torture to the death penalty to the right to health.[35] While simply institutionalizing norms in international law and institutions does not guarantee changes in behavior, in many cases as well, these international laws contributed to behavioral change (Pinker, 2011; Simmons, 2009).

---

[35] See, for example, Hathaway and Shapiro (2017); Inal (2013); Kang (2012); Kinsella (2011); Linde (2016); Nadelmann (1990); Price (1998, 1997); Towns (2010).

### 5.3.1 Transnational Reasoning's Elective Affinity for Some Moral Foundations over Others

We think incorporating findings from IR research on transnationally shared moral norms can often provide a more sanguine view of morality as a progressive versus divisive force at a macro level than approaches which have focused on explaining domestic political value conflict through the psychological level like Haidt's or Greene's. For example, a closer look at the history of international law on moral issues calls into question the proposition that moral positions are mostly driven by intuitions, with some room for reasoned persuasion. While this may be persuasive with regard to individual moral choices, it does not describe the process of debating international moral norms and institutionalizing them into law.

Intuitions, including intuitions about rights, may indeed be part of the automatic system, but transnational norms and international law, while initially motivated by moral intuitions, cannot advance without the manual mode – the hard negotiating of a treaty – having to make arguments that are persuasive to groups of different cultures and backgrounds. This points to a key potential proviso in too-readily applying moral intuitionist approaches to IR, where the relevant agents are anything but novices reacting to carefully designed prompts in a survey. They are much more typically professional politicians, members of international or nongovernmental organizations or otherwise committed activists and the like, often involved in lengthy situations of complex interactions rather than one-off reactions to a given provocative statement about which they may have little knowledge or experience. In this regard, Narvaez importantly has found that the "well-educated intuition of experts is far different from naive intuition, incorporating far more sophisticated, unconscious deep and automatized knowledge that may have been painfully learned from rules" (Narvaez, 2010, p. 171). This presages the possibility that those with expertise in political morality should not necessarily be understood to reason in the same way as the general public, let alone as prone to the same tendencies in actual politics as random subjects in psychological experiments. This would seem to loop us closer back to some of the findings in the IR literature regarding the role that reasoned persuasion can play in complex iterated negotiations (Deitelhoff, 2009; Risse, 2000).

Without minimizing the antics of politics that often take place in such venues, diplomatic meetings may provide just the kind of setting needed for the hard process of reasoning through complex moral issues to take place. As we have seen, effortful reasoning and the concentration and focus it requires does not come naturally to the human brain. Important in that regard is the availability of proper environments for such activity to take place free from the countless distractions that easily disrupt it – that is precisely what libraries and classrooms provide, and so too conference venues for diplomacy (Heath, 2014, pp. 76–77). Diplomats are people too, and thus subject to powerful intuitions that may drive many of their moral views, as well as to their professional obligations to represent the positions of their countries. But the extended time and appropriate spaces of extended negotiations offers a different dynamic for moral views to develop into complex policy responses. This is just the kind of path suggested in IR by Thomas Risse, among others, as a pathway for persuasion in world politics, and the subject of empirical research by a number of IR scholars (Deitelhoff, 2009; Deitelhoff and Müller, 2005; Risse, 2000). Deitelhoff and Müller (2005) found it very challenging empirically to disentangle the extent to which genuine persuasion, arguing, or bargaining prevailed in a given diplomatic setting, but did not suggest that these meeting were mainly based on exchanges of moral intuitions. Armed with the insights of moral psychology, however, Traven, akin to Holmes, argues a key mechanism is that "face-to-face argumentative proceedings require individuals to take the perspective of others and to express their ideas impartially: In diplomatic proceedings, actors use cognitive and emotional heuristics to design the norms of armed conflict" (Traven, 2015, p. 570).

In these settings of international and transnational moral reasoning, drawing on MFT but moving beyond it, we expect that norms about care/harm and fairness have been, and will be more likely to prevail than those connected to obedience, loyalty, and sanctity. Why? Because in order to qualify for international norms and law, it must be possible to universalize, and care and fairness norms have been more open to universalization that the more "binding" foundations that are universal in their presence in many cultures, but parochial in their applications. In other words, diplomats often find it difficult to define these binding foundations, and apply them in a neutral way that could be relevant to all countries.

The success of the anti-apartheid campaign and the Convention for the Elimination of All Forms of Racial Discrimination (CERD) that grew out of it are in turn emblematic of the ways in which the universalizing moral foundations facilitated large numbers of states to take action contrary to the prevailing norms of prejudice and racism. Anti-apartheid sentiment was one of the main factors leading Asian and African leaders to spearhead passage of CERD in 1965 to become the second major international human rights treaty (Jensen, 2016). The antidiscrimination frame rested on the moral foundations of fairness and harm. It ran contrary to moral foundations about loyalty to clan and nation, yet it was difficult for countries with racial segregation to find persuasive arguments against the basic claims of CERD. We find the ability of this campaign initiated by social movements and supported initially by weak recently decolonized states, to be an example of the argument we make about the greater ability to universalize norms grounded in fairness and harm moral foundations and successfully institutionalize them within the UN system.

The Russian campaign for "traditional values" in the UN Human Rights Council provides a more current illustration of both the role of intuition and the parochial moral foundations in international politics, and yet the difficulty of moving these intuitions toward international norms and law by a process that involves engaging in moral reasoning and persuasion. This is a clear example of an attempt by a powerful state actor, backed by a transnational religious movement, to use sanctity and authority moral foundations to develop new international norms. A study by Russian academics clarifies that the traditional values resolutions were intended to challenge resolutions in the UN HR Council on LGBT rights (Semenova et al., 2015).

Russia first presented Human Rights Council resolution 16/3, calling for the preparation of a study on "how a better understanding and appreciation of traditional values of dignity, freedom and responsibility can contribute to the promotion and protection of human rights" (UN Human Rights Council Advisory Committee, 2012). With regard to the moral intuitions, the resolution pressed lots of buttons; by speaking of tradition, dignity, freedom, and responsibility, it engaged the liberal, conservative, and even libertarian foundations. Twenty-four member countries of the Human Rights Council voted in favor of the resolution, fourteen against, and seven abstained, some of whom may have been voting their intuitions. But when the Advisory Committee members undertook the mandated study, they had to move beyond the moral intuitions and begin the hard work of moral reasoning. Their final report reveals what a slow process of moral reasoning looked like. The Advisory Committee final report noted, first, that there is "no agreed definition of the term 'traditional values of humankind,'" nor did such a definition result from the discussions held by the Human Rights Council or the Advisory Committee (UN Human Rights Council Advisory Committee, 2012). Next, the Advisory Committee pointed out that "Human rights have moral universality, since human rights are held universally by all persons 'simply because one is a human being,' and international normative universality, meaning that human rights are universally accepted by Governments through their commitments and obligations under international human rights law." The report noted, however, that "traditions are so varied and complex that, while some traditions comply with human rights norms and contribute to their promotion and protection, others undermine or are in conflict with them."

Faced with these obstacles, Russia tried another angle and pushed forward a second resolution asking for another report on best practices of incorporating traditional values into human rights work (United Nations Human Rights Council Resolution 21/3, 2012). The subsequent report on best practices that the Russians requested "displays the weaknesses of the entire traditional values agenda" (Horsfjord, 2016). The Russians did not really want to know about best practices from traditional values from around the world, as evidenced by their failure to submit their own list of best practices. They were interested instead in promoting the agenda of the Russian Orthodox Church, as one way to enhance the position of Russia as a force in international politics that offered an alternative to the West. The Russian Orthodox Church authorities later met with Islamic religious leaders, but in the end, it seems that when they said traditional values, they meant the values of their own religion. "The values promoted by other traditions are recognized as traditional values to the extent that they accord with those discerned from one's own source of authority" (Horsfjord, 2016, p. 75). One problem with all authority-based moral foundations is that they cannot easily be universalized; they are not about respecting authority in general, but respecting one's own source of authority, and other authorities are recognized only so far as their values as similar to those of one's own authorities. In fast intuitive thinking these arguments to traditional values may appeal, but they are parochial, and when you get to slow negotiation of language, it turns out that it is difficult to persuade others who do not embrace your particular authority figures and traditions to join you. The resolutions received some significant support from Council members, but when faced with the diplomatic work of deliberation, the binding moral instincts were not enough to carry the day. The campaign has not yet led to changes in transnational norms, or international law, and is unlikely to do so.

### 5.3.2 What Is the Metamorality: Rights or Utilitarianism?

This then leads us to a point we would like to make in response to Greene's argument that a utilitarian approach is most characteristic of the manual (slow) mode of moral reasoning, while deontological ethics like human rights and Kantian moral rules are typically driven by moral intuitions. Greene further says that the kind of reasoning we need is to develop a "metamorality" – a higher-level moral system that allows us to adjudicate among the moralities of different moral tribes. He rejects the idea of the cultural relativist, as do we, that there is no right answer, that "each tribe will do it their own way." But Greene also rejects the idea that there is a metamorality of rights out there to be rationally discovered, as distinct from being established. Instead he proposes "the splendid idea" that utilitarianism could be the metamorality we need.

Kahane has argued that Greene's own evidence cannot sustain such claims, and that the best that can be said based on the evidence, including Kahane's own fMRI experiments, is that "Intuitive judgments are generally associated with automatic processing, and counterintuitive judgments with controlled processing," but the latter need not at all be utilitarian (Kahane, 2012, p. 540). As the history of human rights treaty negotiation and the previous example show from the perspective of IR research, the slow manual mode of reasoning has been used frequently and effectively with regard to deontological human rights claims.

Empirically, IR norms theorists have long demonstrated that the globe is no longer a tabula rasa onto which we can project a new metamorality, but rather a place where activists and diplomats have already been developing a metamorality for a couple of centuries and institutionalizing it in international law. This includes, among many other developments, the abolition of piracy and slavery in the nineteenth century and the development of laws of war and the creation of the human rights regime in the twentieth century. Nor, by the second half of the twentieth century, was this metamorality imposed by the so-called civilized states on the rest of the world. International human rights norms and law were drafted in deeply deliberative processes with all existing states in the world and ample input from NGOs and later refined and interpreted through the work of expert quasi-judicial and judicial bodies like the Human Rights Committee or the Inter-American Court of Human Rights. Like Charles Beitz (2009), we believe that existing human rights law is a good place to begin our moral inquiry because the multiple decisions of many individuals and states around the world seems a better ethical starting place than to substitute our own normative criteria.

This existing global metamorality *has* been based on moral intuitions, especially rights and fairness, but has used hard reasoning and deliberation to move beyond intuitions into a negotiated, agreed upon moral and legal framework, to which countries can later consent through ratification, and reservations of the relevant treaties, and that can be further refined by judicial and quasi-judicial interpretations. These interpretations do make hard calls about trade-offs, but they often do so within a framework of rights, rather than outside of one. In this sense, we come down on the side of Stephen Pinker that the rights revolution has provided a metamorality mainly as the result of the application of reason. But to defend and extend that rights revolution requires the continued and insistent application of emotion, reason, and activism.

Specifically, if it is the case that liberal moral foundations have been more frequently included in international law and international institutions, what does this mean for thinking about moral foundations? Could it be the case that because the harm and fairness moral foundations are those that are most likely to be shared by both liberals and conservatives, they form the basis for international agreements? Could it be that these international institutions have a built-in bias for liberalism, and thus are more open to care and fairness arguments and less open to the binding foundations?

The global rights revolution began when the world was not majority democratic, so it reflected the moral aspirations of societies, not their then-current form of government. The binding foundations, while widely shared, are by nature more parochial – both obedience to authority and the loyalty are inevitably owed to local or national leaders and clans; sanctity is to local religious thought. These more parochial moral foundations do not lend themselves as well to serving as transnational norms or international law. The one big exception, of course, is loyalty and obedience to the nation-state, which now spans the globe and is more widely shared perhaps than any other moral foundation. The nation-state continues to be at the center of all international law. That has always been a taken-for-granted fact in IR, so none of us will be surprised to recognize the continuing power that the grip of these "imagined communities" has on the morality of the world. We see it strongly, for example, as a counterbalance to concerns about harm and fairness in international law with regard to refugees and migrants. What surprises us is how such law has changed over the last century to also include many more concerns about care/harm, fairness, and even liberty, despite the ongoing centrality of the state and loyalty and obedience to it.

## 6 Prescriptions for Advocacy

Moral norms never succeed by themselves, but only when they are taken up by well-organized campaigns, capable of compelling framing, persuasion, and pressure. But on those issues where powerful moral intuitions come into conflict with one another, there is a need for even more culturally sensitive campaigns and careful framing that will appeal to common moral foundations and overcome or neutralize opposition, or at least not trigger it.

Some of the issues and research discussed here have practical implications for advocacy. For example, to the extent liberals and conservatives process moral information differently, advocacy strategies that make the most sense to advocates themselves may often in fact be falling upon mostly deaf ears among those they most want to change. Advocacy groups might be advised to have multiple strategies for different audiences. Feinberg and Willer tested this hypothesis, finding that "Arguments that appeal to one's own moral convictions may resonate with those who ascribe to a similar political ideology (because they share similar moral values), but these arguments are likely unconvincing to those with a differing political ideology (because they do not share the same moral convictions)" (Feinberg and Willer, 2015, pp. 1–3).

This is more problematic when people espousing different moral values are defined as beyond the pale of persuasion, as is sometimes the case for the debates on immigration in the United States and Europe. For Haidt,

> whether you are a status quo conservative concerned about rapid change or an authoritarian who is hypersensitive to normative threat, high levels of Muslim immigration into your Western nation are likely to threaten your core moral concerns. But as soon as you speak up to voice those concerns, globalists will scorn you as a racist . . . .. These actions press the "normative threat" button in the minds of those who are predisposed to authoritarianism, and these actions can drive status quo conservatives to join authoritarians in fighting back against the globalists and their universalistic projects. (Haidt, 2016)

Haidt's moral psychology leads him to the conclusion that immigration policies should admit low numbers (or if moderate levels, immigrants who are assimilationist), otherwise immigration will be guaranteed to provoke a backlash. Yet, in the end, this analysis misses the critical link of politics in our view and thus draws inadequately supported conclusions and policy recommendations. There is variation across countries in how immigrants are received; it is not as if one particular numeric threshold automatically ignites this or that reaction due to individual psychology. Canada took in proportionately a far higher number of Syrian refugees than the United States at the height of the exodus around 2015–16, without significant backlash nor without igniting a powerful populist movement. One factor helping explain these different moral responses to providing refuge for those fleeing war was that such refugees were not successfully securitized in Canada the way they were by opponents of migration in the United States, starting at the top with then–candidate and eventual president Donald Trump who equated them with criminals and terrorists. Numerous scholars have documented the processes of securitization of immigration to help explain variation in migration policies across countries (Bourbeau, 2011; Watson, 2009), and it is such political dynamics that provide a critical link between these important psychological responses and policy. More broadly, then, comparing and synthesizing findings from IR scholars and psychologists on such important issues promises more comprehensive accounts than focusing on the individual level or domestic/transnational levels alone.

## 6.1 Framing

The most important framing take-away from this research is that activists need to frame appeals in language that may trigger new intuitions on the other side (Haidt and Joseph, 2004).

The diversity of moral instincts reinforces our sense that this is not only a story about idealism versus self-interest, but one where different types of moral instincts often come into conflict with one another, so that the political strategies and framing of movements can be essential to help new ideas and norms succeed. Issue characteristics are not a feature completely separate from agents; sometimes activists and other agents are aware of these intrinsic issue characteristics and engage in strategic social construction by trying to choose and frame issues that will most appeal to emotion and moral instincts. The activists who launched the Nestle Boycott wanted to organize an anti-corporate campaign. Knowing that it would be a tough sell in a capitalist society, they choose an issue involving bodily harm to a vulnerable group – the babies who died from "bottle-baby" disease caused by corporate marketing of infant formula to poor families without access to clean water (Sikkink, 1986).

Likewise, because conservatives tend to value social order and stability, Haidt argues that framing gay marriage as helping people to form life-long commitments that will often create stability for children may be more effective than talking about fairness (Haidt and Joseph, 2004, pp. 65–66). This assumes, of course, that the purpose of framing is gaining support from as many people as possible. For some social movements, the purpose of framing their issues may be to define their identity and gatekeep the boundaries of that identity, in which case this advice will be irrelevant. But some campaigns, aware of these issues, have made concerted efforts to tailor their messages to attracting new constituencies. For example, the campaign that eventually led to the acceptance of gay marriage in the United States was very conscious of trying to reach out to new groups. They discovered that messages from well-known actors or sports figures stressing family and community were more likely to gather support and resonated more than abstract appeals for rights.

As a result of this research, we also recognize that unnecessarily complex messages requiring the hard work of sustained reasoning may be disadvantaged compared to powerful emotional appeals that engage intuitive cognitive processing. Drawing upon psychology, philosopher Joseph Heath has brilliantly dissected the reasons why many progressive solutions to complex policy problems are frankly difficult to explain, while simplistic slogans that reach the heart, not the brain, so often seem to win the day (Heath, 2014).

The norms literature that has been premised upon processes of persuasion and pressure needs to come to grips with how such factors affect the uptake of advocacy campaign techniques specifically, and other attempts to foster change more generally. Heath and Haidt, among others, have made the case for how this has played to the advantage of conservatives in the United States in recent decades who have been better at simplistic framings of issues in ways that stick with the hearts of the public. The problem is that many complex political issues require nuanced positions, yet those who go that route are mocked, like John Kerry was in running for US president for being "nuancy boy." Some issues are inherently complex and many policy proposals of liberals are more difficult to frame in ways that intuitively resonate as well as the simple messages of their opponents. Thus, calls for greater punishments for criminals whether for the war on drugs, illegal immigrants, or even support for torture for terrorists appeal to the powerful impulse for retribution of wrongs, yet experts know such policies are usually not as effective as they may feel to some people (Heath, 2014, pp. 253–254).

Feinberg and Willer's research has clear implications for advocates being very self-conscious about the psychology of their framing strategies. For instance, advocates for climate change action, instead of appealing to frames of global equity or fairness, would be better advised to stress connections to local conservation/reverence for status quo that after all lies at the core of conservative beliefs, though that seems to have been forgotten in much political discourse in contemporary times as climate politics has often become polarized into bipartisan camps. Putting these ideas to the test, Feinberg and Willer found that "conservatives demonstrated greater support for pro-environmental legislation when advocacy statements were framed in terms of the more conservative value of purity than those presented with arguments framed in terms of the more liberal value of harm or a control" (Feinberg and Willer, 2015, p. 1667). Similarly, Kidwell, Farmer, and Hardesty found that presenting pro-environment arguments couched in terms of loyalty, authority, and purity increased the likelihood that conservatives would recycle, and found that these effects persisted over a fourteen-week period (Kidwell et al., 2013). Together, these studies suggest moral reframing can serve as an effective means for promoting pro-environmental attitudes and behaviors in conservatives.

What about fear? Climate change would seem to be a prime candidate for a politics of fear that tends to resonate with conservatives. Interestingly, some pro-climate change activists, including the iconic Al Gore, have veered away from messages of fear lately, wary that apocalyptic messages may be inducing resignation, defensive avoidance, and paralysis in terms of political action. But we have seen that conservative tend to be particularly prone to fear stimuli, a finding that seems to accord well with conservative and radical-right messaging around migrants and terrorists. Why have such messages around climate not tapped into conservatives politics of fear? Some psychologists postulate that such powerful intuitions can be overridden by tribal loyalties; thus as Kahan has interpreted, conservatives are trying to manage their own more limited social environment rather than the earth's environment (Greene, 2013, p. 92). In the case of climate change in the United States, "the two parties diverged on climate change because this issue *got politicized*, forcing some people to choose between being informed by experts and being good members of their tribe" (Greene, 2013, p. 95). That is, when issues "become tribal badges of honor . . . [they] are very difficult to change, and changing them is no longer simply a matter of educating people" (Greene, 2013, p. 94). This is most interesting, as it suggests that the politics of identity can come first. An implication, then, is that for some issues, the key for a campaign that can effectively reach a broad audience is for it *not* to be politicized, by that we mean specifically in partisan terms. Here IR findings can provide a useful bridge. Research on campaigns on female genital cutting in Africa, for example, has discovered that community level factors stressing local NGO participation and values has been more successful than top-down naming and shaming (Cloward, 2016; Mackie, 1996). Similarly, Kristi Kenyon examined the effects of framing HIV/AIDS advocacy as a human rights issue versus public health, finding that in some societies where rights language was prominent, like South Africa, the rights frame was a good fit, whereas it was regarded with more suspicion in places like Botswana (Kenyon, 2017).

## 6.2 Communication in the Social Media Environment

We know that media has an effect in shaping people's opinions including on moral issues. These tendencies are exacerbated in contemporary times due to the social media environment, in which we are routinely bombarded with types and volumes of messages that overwhelm our brain's innate capacities and thus ability to process, and that play to a number of biases which impede rational solutions to political problems (Heath, 2014).

But understanding just how stimuli affect the very structure of the brain can be initially quite disconcerting. As Jost and colleagues put it, "at this point one can only guess about the neurological consequences of watching Fox News or PBS Newshour for years at a time, but evidence from cognitive neuroscience suggests that repeated experiences may be capable of altering the structures and functions of the human brain" (Jost et al., 2014, p. 30). Several pathological effects of the information environment are accentuated by the overwhelming nature of the social media and its selectivity in what people receive.

In the natural environment of evolutionary adaptation, the only way to see something happen was for it to actually happen to you or someone near you. In an age of media and images, however, we can see something again and again even when it has only happened once, but the brain unconsciously logs another occurrence each time (Heath, 2014). The resulting availability heuristic means that our intuitions about how often things occur are extremely unreliable as we judge those probabilities on the basis of the ease with which such events are recalled, not their actual likelihood (Tversky and Kahneman, 1973). And yet, these repeated messages can be incredibly effective as advertisers and political operators alike have long appreciated. The banal if sad truth of the "illusory truth effect" is that people are more likely to believe something to be true the more often they hear it, regardless of its veracity, which goes for moral advocacy messages as much as any others. In politics, this includes manifest falsehoods, and messages that appeal more strongly to the gut and how people feel rather than their reason. The world itself is an ever-increasingly complex environment, which

> places increasing demands on our rational faculties – increasing our cognitive load, requiring us to pay more attention and exercise greater effort. We find ourselves constantly having to override our natural impulses in order to think things through more carefully. Reason, however, is subject to bottlenecks, and attention is an intrinsically scarce resource. So, it is inevitable that as our environment becomes more unnatural, we begin to see a degradation of cognitive performance. (Heath, 2014, p. 168)

This is quite a different picture from the initial promise of the internet and social media as a potential source of power for the people, including members of civil society working through transnational advocacy networks for humanitarian causes. IR scholarship has shown how social media did enable some advocacy campaigns, including the diffusion of the Arab Spring activism from one country to another, as well as its uses to protesters on the ground (Aday et al., 2013, p. 904), or the campaign for the arrest of Joseph Kony, the leader of the Ugandan Lord's Resistance Army (LRA), for war crimes and recruiting child soldiers. But later, social media became polarizing in the Arab Spring, as Islamic groups and their adversaries retreated into their respective social media camps where they reinforced their prejudices ("Arab Spring: Did social media really spark revolutions?," 2013).

The tide has turned and social media is under scrutiny for its role in a variety of efforts to undermine international norms such as the role of Facebook being used to facilitate genocide in Myanmar, and state-based propaganda trying to sow confusion around the violation of international norms such as Syria's and Russia's efforts to accuse anyone but the Syrian regime of violations of the chemical weapons taboo.

The takeaways for advocacy, similar to the issue of framing above, is about the need to learn how to escape from using social media as an echo chamber of already committed activists, and seek out ways to use it as a tool to attract new constituencies. Psychological research does not offer any silver bullets here, except to stress that one's opponents may also be making moral arguments, just different types of moral arguments, and that their brains may be prewired to be receptive to appeals to different kinds of moral intuitions.

Advocacy strategies with social media are compounded by research finding that lies spread faster than truth online. A study of rumor cascades on Twitter found that false news reached many more people than the truth; "the top 1% of false news cascades diffused to between 1000 and 100,000 people, whereas the truth rarely diffused to more than 1000 people" (Vosoughi et al., 2018). False news was seen as more novel but also inspired more fear and disgust, so moral intuitions may be responsible for the faster spread of false news.

In this situation, framing and social media advocacy campaigns looking to counter misinformation would be well advised to follow a recommendation cognitive linguist Geoff Lakoff made to journalists in the post-truth era, to present material in a "truth sandwich." You should never repeat the lie or even use the language of the lie, this only aids its growth. Instead, "first tell the truth; then you point out what the lie is and how it diverges from the truth. Then you repeat the truth and tell the consequences of the difference between the truth and the lie" (Illing, 2019).

Given research discussed in Section 3.6.1 about the potential effects of empathetic distress, messaging also needs to make sure it does not provoke burnout or a desire to withdraw from a situation. Excessively negative communications about crisis and threat may provoke at least some minds to turn off the message rather than engage. Some researchers and practitioners now argue for more "hope-based" communication that energizes advocacy rather than provokes withdrawal. Nabi et al. for example showed that climate change messages "that evoked the most hope were associated with more supportive attitudes and advocacy" (Nabi et al., 2018, p. 460). Former Amnesty International communications director Thomas Coombes has been so persuaded by the psychological literature on the need for more positive messaging that he now advocates a "hope based communication strategy," drawing on the work of Lakoff and many others. The strategy calls for five shifts that advocacy groups need to make: (1) talk about solutions, not problems; (2) highlight what you stand for, not what you oppose; (3) create opportunities, drop threats; (4) emphasize support for heroes, not victims; and (5) emphasize the thrill of victories.[36] Further research should investigate the results.

---

[36] See "A Guide to Hope-Based Communications": www.openglobalrights.org/hope-guide/.

## 6.3 Training and Education

Neuroplasticity provides part of the neurological underpinning of research findings that with education, training, and experience, what once required effortful reasoning can become intuitive. While it is "only very recently that neuroscience began to investigate the neural plasticity underlying our capacity for empathy and compassion"; studies have found that

> short-term compassion training of several days was able to increase positive affect and activations in a neural network usually related to positive emotions ... [and] several days of empathy training led to an activation increase in insula and anterior middle cingulate cortex, as well as to an increase in self-reported negative affect. In contrast, subsequent compassion training in the same participants could reverse this effect by decreasing negative affect and increasing positive affect. (Singer and Klimecki, 2014, p. 877)

Jost notes that "compassion training alters neural responses in the anterior cingulate and anterior insula – brain regions that are associated with empathy in response to the pain of others" (Jost et al., 2014, p. 30).

While studies of the effects of empathy or compassion training have found positive results, other studies have found that limited training has a short shelf life, which is consistent with neuroplasticity. After a brief period of practice, like cramming for a test, it is relatively easy to improve in some domains as we strengthen existing synaptic connections; but we also tend to quickly forget what we have crammed – because they are easy-come, easy-go neuronal connections and are rapidly reversed. Maintaining improvement and making a skill permanent require the slow steady work that probably forms new connections; sustained practice is needed to solidify learning (Doidge, 2007, pp. 199–200).

This would seem to dovetail with, among other things, virtue theories of ethics. Virtue ethics, famously articulated by Aristotle, counsels the cultivation of skills and practical wisdom through experience and the practice of valued virtues like judgment, empathy, discernment, and reason (Cameron, 2018, pp. 14–16). Indeed, some think that virtue ethics is the approach that best maps onto the reality of how people actually psychologically do morality (Haidt and Joseph, 2004). These findings should help us recognize the limits of a cerebral route to moral education based mainly on clarifying rules and principles. To fully grasp a moral education, children need to be immersed in environments that are "rich in stories and examples that adults interpret with emotion. Those stories and examples should trigger the innate moral modules, if possible, and link them to broader virtues and principles" (Haidt and Joseph, 2004, p. 65).

In the current era of backlash, the transnational environment can be hostile to the cultivation of liberal international norms, without replacing them with other norms for reasons indicated earlier. We thus expect that contemporary authoritarian and parochial rejections of liberal internationalism will not result in new global conservative norms or law as such, so much as simply a retreat to a more stripped-down and thin global normative order dominated more by parochial sovereign prerogatives.

# 7 Conclusions

Since the zenith of the debates between rationalism and constructivism as antipodes in IR, there has emerged a prevalent post-constructivist/rationalist view that both the strategic and moral are typically at play to varying degrees in political action (Checkel, 2013; Fearon and Wendt, 2002). This view, which we think is a progressive advance following from IR research, was a result of an effort by constructivists to show that the more exclusivist claims of skeptical traditions – that morality does not matter in world politics – are not valid; constructivists, among other scholars, have been successful in empirically demonstrating that sometimes transnational morality does have a meaningful impact in world politics.

But constructivists were still far from understanding how and why, and under what conditions, morality has an impact on world politics. In this Element, we have attempted to canvas recent research in neuroscience and moral psychology and its emerging IR applications in order to harness their insights more pointedly for our understanding of international norms. We propose a future research agenda building on these developments and taking them to the next level to address long-standing issues and unanswered questions in the field of norms research. Indeed, the major premise of this Element is that there are far broader and potentially profound possibilities now than ever for the psychological microfoundational and also moral contextual grounds for our understanding of norms.

To summarize the research prescriptions we discuss in this Element, we stress that a greater understanding of moral psychology and neuroscience would assist norms researchers in answering some of our own most pressing issues about the origins of norms and why some norms win out over others. First, IR norms researchers need to overcome their embrace of the blank-slate model of cognition, which can no longer be sustained in light of advances in psychological and neuroscience research. Next, IR norms researchers will benefit from becoming more open-minded and curious consumers of psychological research, at the same time as we recognize its limitations to help us answer questions about dynamic changes in transnational norms. By encouraging researchers to study both the universalizing and parochial moral foundations in MFT, including loyalty, authority, and sanctity as sources of transnational norm campaigns, we can understand that individuals are motivated by a wider variety of moralities. Second, a clearer understanding of the dual processing brain would help norm researchers situate their work about the different ways norms emerge and resonate vis both an intuitive and emotional "System 1" and a deliberative "System 2." Such an understanding could help norms researchers and IR scholars realize that what are often taken for moral justifications for deeper interests may actually be intuitive and emotional moral reactions of System 1 brain processes.

Theoretical and empirical considerations of morality in IR have often focused on the role played by the rational persuasion of others by the best argument. And yet, a substantial body of contemporary work in psychology and neuroscience finds that moral values tend to be more driven by instinct, intuition, and emotion than rational cognition and persuasion as such. We do not argue that reason and logic are absent or irrelevant for norms debates. Indeed, there is an interesting preponderance of mutual acknowledgment among neuroscientists and IR scholars that it is mistaken to frame these issues in terms of a dichotomy between emotion and/or intuition and reason, insofar as they are inextricably intertwined in cognition. Psychologists and neuroscientists are confirming that, as Hume noted long ago, there is no moral reason without emotion (Jeffery, 2014). But that does not mean that reason plays no part in social and political moral progress, quite the contrary. Indeed psychologist Steven Pinker's assessment of vast interdisciplinary research has led him to argue persuasively that ultimately it is reason that is the primary motor of moral progress (Pinker, 2011). Accordingly, among scholars and segments of the policy community, arguments based on reason, logic, argument, and persuasion will continue to be necessary and important.[37] This is in line with our argument that while all the moral foundations are present in transnational advocacy, intuitions about care/harm and fairness, along with the ever-present parochial loyalty to the nation-state, have been more deeply institutionalized in international law, and it is largely as a result of reasoned deliberation that these moral arguments have been and can be universalized.

Finally, this approach can help IR norms scholars revisit the agent–structure debate from a different angle. It provides the microfoundations for global norms of stability and change by helping us understand the interactions between

---

[37] See, for example, Gallagher (2013). Gallagher argues that explanations based on one type of emotional appeal (altruism) have failed, and that we need justifications based on reason and logic.

individual moral instincts and the situational and cultural context within which agents make decisions, which in turn can influence intuitions. Norms researchers could use a wide variety of research methods and techniques to test such hypotheses, including qualitative case studies with process tracing, discourse analysis, interviews, historical comparative analysis, fuzzy-set qualitative comparative analysis, or surveys and survey experiments.

Our research has implications as well for advocacy. If instead of appealing to reason, advocates mainly seek to foster their own emotional appeals, the challenge is that we cannot rely just on empathy as a strong emotion to build a better world. Pinker has argued, for example, "The problem with building a better world through empathy, in the sense of contagion, mimicry, vicarious emotion, or mirror neurons, is that it cannot be counted on to trigger the kind of empathy we want, namely sympathetic concern for others' well-being" (Pinker, 2011, p. 580). For Pinker, empathy is too parochial to serve as a force for universal consideration of people's interests; mirror neurons notwithstanding. Rather it is turned on by cuteness, good looks, kinship, friendship, similarity, and communal solidarity. While it can be spread outward by taking other people's perspectives, the increments are small and likely to be ephemeral. Similarly, Mercer (2014) has noted that while there is no upper limit to identification, those who identify with all of humanity seem to be comparatively rare. Yet as Haidt (2016) notes, the World Values Surveys run since the 1980s show that as societies grow wealthier, "nations move away from 'survival values' emphasizing the economic and physical security found in one's family, tribe, and other parochial groups, toward 'self-expression' or 'emancipative values' that emphasize individual rights and protections – not just for oneself, but as a matter of principle, for everyone." Thus Pinker argues that "What really has expanded is not so much a circle of empathy as a circle of rights – a commitment that other living things, no matter how distant or dissimilar, be safe from harm and exploitation." What is needed, that is, are policies and norms that become second nature and render empathy unnecessary (Pinker, 2011, pp. 591–592). Human rights around the world continue to be violated because people are excluded from this circle of rights, this realm of obligation of others to respect rights. If we are to move from a circle of empathy to a circle of rights, it involves an expansion of the realm of obligation to include all humans (Fein, 1993). Promoting such a goal will require not only a combination of emotion and reason but the very best strategies and tactics to effectively communicate with people with whom we disagree at the intuitive level. The norms research agenda we propose here would not only advance theory in our field, but also provide an intellectual underpinning to this goal. In short, a collaborative conversation between moral psychologists, neuroscientists, and social scientists, among others, is a necessary step for this complex challenge.

# References

Acharya, A., 2004. How ideas spread: whose norms matter? norm localization and institutional change in Asian Regionalism. *Int. Organ.* 58, 239–275.

Aday, S., Farrell, H., Freelon, D., Lynch, M., Sides, J., Dewar, M., 2013. Watching from afar: media consumption patterns around the Arab Spring. *Am. Behav. Sci.* 57, 899–919.

Adler, E., Pouliot, V., 2011. *International practices.* Cambridge University Press, New York.

Alcock, J., 2001. *The triumph of sociobiology.* Oxford University Press, Oxford; New York.

"Arab Spring: did social media really spark revolutions?," 2013. Middle East Online. https://middle-east-online.com/en/arab-spring-did-social-media-really-spark-revolutions (accessed 5.2.20).

Arendt, H., 2006. *Eichmann in Jerusalem: a report on the banality of evil,* Penguin classics. Penguin Books, New York.

Asch, S. E., 1951. Effects of group pressure on the modification and distortion of judgments, in Guetzkow, H. (ed.), *Groups, leadership and men.* Carnegie Press, Pittsburgh, pp. 177–190.

Bakker, B. N., Schumacher, G., Gothreau, C., Arceneaux, K., 2020. Conservatives and liberals have similar physiological responses to threats. *Nat. Hum. Behav.* 1–9.

Bandes, S., Salerno, J., 2014. Emotion, proof and prejudice: the cognitive science of gruesome photos and victim impact statements. *Arizona State Law Journal* 46, 1006–1056.

Barkow, J. H., Cosmides, L., Tooby, J., 1995. *The adapted mind: evolutionary psychology and the generation of culture.* Oxford University Press.

Batson, C. D., 2009. These things called empathy: eight related but distinct phenomena, in Decety, J., Ickes, W. (eds), *The social neuroscience of empathy.* The MIT Press, Cambridge, MA, pp.1–15.

Bayram, A. B., 2017. Due deference: cosmopolitan social identity and the psychology of legal obligation in international politics. *Int. Organ.* 71, S137–S163.

Bayram, A., Holmes, M., 2020. Feeling their pain: affective empathy and public preferences for foreign development aid. *Euro J of Inter Rel.* 26, 820–850.

Beitz, C. R., 2009. *The idea of human rights.* Oxford University Press, Oxford; New York.

Bennett, A., Checkel, J. T., 2014. *Process tracing*. Cambridge University Press, West Nyack.

Berenguer, J. 2010. The effect of empathy in environmental moral reasoning. *Environment and Behavior.* 42, 110–134.

Betts, A., Orchard, P., 2014. *Implementation and world politics: how international norms change practice*, 1st. ed. Oxford University Press, Oxford, UK.

Bloom, P., 2016. The perils of empathy. *Wall Str. J.* http://www.wsj.com/articles/the-perils-of-empathy-1480689513 (accessed 1.04.21).

Bloom, P., 2013. *Just babies: the origins of good and evil*, 1st ed. Crown Publishers, New York.

Bob, C., 2013. The global right wing and theories of transnational advocacy. *Int. Spect.* 48, 71–85.

Bob, C., 2012. *The Global Right Wing and the clash of world politics*, Cambridge studies in contentious politics. Cambridge University Press, New York.

Bourbeau, P., 2011. *The securitization of migration: a study of movement and order.* Routledge, London.

Boyd, R., Richerson, P. J., 1985. *Culture and the evolutionary process*. University of Chicago Press, Chicago.

Bull, H., 1977. *The anarchical society: a study of order in world politics*. Columbia University Press, New York.

Cameron, M. A., 2018. *Political institutions and practical wisdom: between rules and practice*. Oxford University Press.

Checkel, J. T., 2013. Theoretical pluralism in IR: possibilities and limits, in Carlsnaes, W., Risse, T., Simmons, B. (eds.), *Handbook of international relations*. 2nd ed. Sage Publications, London, pp. 220–242.

Checkel, J. T., 1999. Norms, institutions, and national identity in contemporary Europe. *Int. Stud. Q.* 43, 84–114.

Clifford, S., Jerit, J., Rainey, C., Motyl, M., 2015. Moral concerns and policy attitudes: investigating the influence of elite rhetoric. *Polit. Commun.* 32, 229–248.

Cloward, K., 2016. *When norms collide: local responses to activism against female genital mutilation and early marriage*. Oxford University Press, New York.

Cohen, I. G., Daniels, N., Eyal, N. M., Adler, M. D., 2015. *Identified versus statistical lives: an interdisciplinary perspective*, 1st ed. Population-level bioethics series. Oxford University Press, New York.

Crawford, N., 2014. Institutionalizing passion in world politics: fear and empathy, *Int. Theory* 6, 535–557.

Crawford, N., 2013. Emotions and international security: Cave! Hic Libido. *Crit. Stud. Secur.* 1, 121–123.

Crawford, N., 2002. *Argument and change in world politics: ethics, decolonization, and humanitarian intervention*, Cambridge studies in international relations. Cambridge University Press, Cambridge, UK; New York.

Crawford, N., 2009. Homo politicus and argument (nearly) all the way down: persuasion in politics. *Perspect. Polit.* 7, 103–124.

Damasio, A. R., 1994. *Descartes' error: emotion, reason, and the human brain.* GP Putnam, New York.

Deitelhoff, N., 2009. The discursive process of legalization: charting islands of persuasion in the ICC case. *Int. Organ.* 63, 33–65.

Deitelhoff, N., Müller, H., 2005. Theoretical paradise – empirically lost? Arguing with Habermas. *Rev. Int. Stud.* 31, 167–179.

Deitelhoff, N., Zimmermann, L., 2019. Norms under challenge: unpacking the dynamics of norm robustness. *J. Glob. Secur. Stud.* 4, 2–17.

Deitelhoff, N., Zimmermann, L., 2018. Things we lost in the fire: how different types of contestation affect the robustness of international norms. *Int. Stud. Rev.* 22, 51–76.

Doidge, N., 2007. *The brain that changes itself: stories of personal triumph from the frontiers of brain science.* Viking, New York.

Duckitt, J., Sibley, C. G., 2010. Personality, ideology, prejudice, and politics: a dual-process motivational model. *J. Pers.* 78, 1861–1894.

Edmonds, D., 2014. *Would you kill the fat man?: the trolley problem and what your answer tells us about right and wrong.* Princeton University Press, Princeton, NJ.

Faulkner, N., 2018. Put yourself in their shoes: Testing empathy's ability to motivate cosmopolitan behavior. *Pol. Psych.* 39, 217–228.

Fearon, J., Wendt, A., 2002. Rationalism v. constructivism: a skeptical view, in Carlsnaes, W., Risse, T., Simmons, B. (eds.), *Handbook of international relations*. Sage Publications, London, pp. 55–72.

Fein, H., 1993. *Genocide: a sociological perspective.* Sage Publications, London; Newbury Park, CA.

Feinberg, M., Willer, R., 2015. From Gulf to Bridge: When Do Moral Arguments Facilitate Political Influence? *Pers. Soc. Psychol. Bull.* 41, 1665–1681.

Finnemore, M., 2003. *The purpose of intervention: changing beliefs about the use of force*, Cornell studies in security affairs. Cornell University Press, Ithaca.

Finnemore, M., 1996. *National interests in international society*, Cornell studies in political economy. Cornell University Press, Ithaca.

Finnemore, M., Sikkink, K., 1998. International norm dynamics and political change. *Int. Organ.* 52, 887–917.

Florini, A., 1996. The evolution of international norms. *Int. Stud. Q.* 40, 363–389.

Gallagher, A., 2013. *Genocide and its threat to contemporary international order*, New security challenges series. Palgrave Macmillan, Basingstoke, Hampshire; New York.

Gintis, H., 2007. A framework for the unification of the behavioral sciences. *Behav. Brain Sci.* 30, 1–16.

Glanville, L., 2016. Self-interest and the distant vulnerable. *Ethics Int. Aff.* 30, 335–353.

Goldgeier, J., Tetlock, P., 2001. Psychology and international relations theory. *Annu. Rev. Polit. Sci.* 4, 67–92.

Graham, J., Haidt, J., Koleva, S., Motyl, M., Iyer, R., Wojcik, S., Ditto, P., 2013. Moral foundations theory: the pragmatic validity of moral pluralism. *Adv. Exp. Soc. Psychol.* 47, 47, 55–130.

Greene, J. D., 2014. Beyond point-and-shoot morality: why cognitive (neuro) science matters for ethics. *Ethics* 124, 695–726.

Greene, J. D., 2013. *Moral tribes: emotion, reason, and the gap between us and them*. The Penguin Press, New York.

Hafner-Burton, E. M., Haggard, S., Lake, D. A., Victor, D. G., 2017. The Behavioral Revolution and International Relations. *Int Org.* 71, S1–S31.

Haidt, J., 2016. When and why nationalism beats globalism. *Am. Interest.* www .the-american-interest.com/2016/07/10/when-and-why-nationalism-beats-globalism/ (accessed 3.04.20).

Haidt, J., 2012. *The righteous mind: why good people are divided by politics and religion*, 1st ed. Pantheon Books, New York.

Haidt, J., 2003. The moral emotions, in Davidson, R. J., Scherer, K. R., Goldsmith, H. H. (eds.), *Handbook of affective sciences*. Oxford University Press, Oxford, pp. 852–870.

Haidt, J., Joseph, C., 2004. Intuitive ethics: how innately prepared intuitions generate culturally variable virtues. *Daedalus* 133, 55–66.

Hall, T. H., 2015. *Emotional diplomacy: official emotion on the international stage*. Cornell University Press, Ithaca.

Hall, T. H., Ross, A. A. G., 2015. Affective politics after 9/11. *Int. Organ.* 69, 847–879.

Hartman, A., Morse, B., 2020. Violence, empathy and altruism: evidence from the Ivorian refugee crisis in Liberia," *British Journal of Political Science* 50, 731–755.

Hathaway, O. A., Shapiro, S. J., 2017. *The internationalists: how a radical plan to outlaw war remade the world*. Simon and Schuster, New York.

Head, N., 2016. A politics of empathy: encounters with empathy in Israel and Palestine. *Review of International Studies*. 42, 95–113.

Heath, J., 2014. *Enlightenment 2.0: restoring sanity to our politics, our economy, and our lives*, 1st ed. HarperCollins, Toronto, Ontario.

Henrich, J. P., 2015. *The secret of our success: how culture is driving human evolution, domesticating our species, and making us smarter.* Princeton University Press, Princeton.

Holmes, M., 2018. *Face-to-face diplomacy: social neuroscience and international relations.* Cambridge University Press, Cambridge.

Holmes, M., 2013. The force of face-to-face diplomacy: mirror neurons and the problem of intentions. *Int. Organ.* 67, 829–861.

Holmes, M., Yarhi-Milo, K., 2017. The psychological logic of peace summits: how empathy shapes outcomes of diplomatic negotiations. *Int. Stud. Q.* 61, 107–122.

Hooper, M., 2016. Russia's 'traditional values' leadership. *Foreign Policy Cent.* https://fpc.org.uk/russias-traditional-values-leadership/ (accessed 4.30.20).

Horowitz, M., Yaworsky, W., Kickham, K., 2014. Whither the blank slate? a report on the reception of evolutionary biological ideas among sociological theorists. *Sociol. Spectr.* 34, 489–509.

Horsfjord, V.L., 2016. Negotiating traditional values: the Russian Orthodox Church at the UN Human Rights Council, in Stensvold, A. (ed.), *Religion, state and the United Nations: value politics*. Routledge, London, pp. 62–78.

Hughes, V., 2014. Emotion is not the enemy of reason. *Natl. Geogr.* www .nationalgeographic.com/science/phenomena/2014/09/18/emotion-is-not-the-enemy-of-reason/ (accessed 4. 30.20).

Hutchinson, E., 2016. *Affective communities in world politics: collective emotions after trauma.* Cambridge University Press, Cambridge.

Illing, S., 2019. How the media should respond to Trump's lies: state of the union edition. *Vox.* www.vox.com/2018/11/15/18047360/trump-state-of-the-union-speech-2019-george-lakoff (accessed 3.04.21).

ILGA, 2020. State-sponsored homophobia report, Latest Edition, https://ilga .org/state-sponsored-homophobia-report (accessed 3.8.21).

Inal, T., 2013. *Looting and rape in wartime: law and change in international relations*, 1st ed. *Pennsylvania studies in human rights*. University of Pennsylvania Press, Philadelphia.

International Commission of Jurists (ICJ), 2007. Yogyakarta Principles – Principles on the application of international human rights law in relation to sexual orientation and gender identity.

Janoff-Bulman, R., Carnes, N.C., 2013. Surveying the moral landscape: moral motives and group-based moralities. *Personal. Soc. Psychol. Rev.* 17, 219–236.

Jeffery, R., 2014. *Reason and emotion in international ethics*. Cambridge University Press, Cambridge.

Jensen, S., 2016. *The making of international human rights: the 1960s, decolonization, and the reconstruction of global values*. Cambridge University Press, New York.

Jervis, R., 1989. Political psychology: some challenges and opportunities. *Polit. Psychol.* 10, 481.

Jost, J. T., Nam, H. H., Amodio, D. M., Van Bavel, J. J., 2014. Political neuroscience: the beginning of a beautiful friendship. *Polit. Psychol.* 35, 3–42.

Kahane, G., 2012. On the wrong track: process and content in moral psychology. *Mind Lang.* 27, 519–545.

Kahneman, D., 2011. *Thinking, fast and slow*, 1st ed., Farrar, Straus and Giroux, New York.

Kang, S.L., 2012. *Human rights and labor solidarity: trade unions in the global economy*, 1st ed., Pennsylvania studies in human rights. University of Pennsylvania Press, Philadelphia.

Katzenstein, P., 1996a. *The culture of national security: norms and identity in world politics*. Columbia University Press, New York.

Katzenstein, P., 1996b. Introduction: alternative perspectives on national security, in Katzenstein, P. (ed.), *The culture of national security: norms and identity in world politics*. Columbia University Press, New York, pp. 1–32.

Keck, M. E., Sikkink, K., 1998. *Activists beyond borders: advocacy networks in international politics*. Cornell University Press, Ithaca.

Kenkel, K. M., Cunliffe, P. (eds.), 2016. *Brazil as a rising power: intervention norms and the contestation of global order*, 1st ed. Routledge, New York.

Kenyon, K., 2017. *Resilience and contagion: invoking human rights in African HIV advocacy*. McGill-Queen's University Press, Montreal.

Keohane, R., 1984. *After hegemony: Cooperation and discord in the world political economy*. Princeton University Press, Princeton.

Kertzer, J., Tingley, D., 2018. Political psychology in international relations: beyond the paradigms. *Annu. Rev. Polit. Sci.* 21, 319.

Kertzer, J. D., 2017. Microfoundations in international relations. *Confl. Manag. Peace Sci.* 34, 81–97.

Kertzer, J. D., Mcgraw, K. M., 2012. Folk realism: testing the microfoundations of realism in ordinary citizens. *Int. Stud. Q.* 56, 245–258.

Kertzer, Joshua D, Powers, K. E., Rathbun, B. C., Iyer, R., 2014. Moral support: how moral values shape foreign policy attitudes *J. Polit.* 76, 825–840.

Kidwell, B., Farmer, A., Hardesty, D. M., 2013. Getting Liberals and Conservatives to go green: political ideology and congruent appeals. *J. Consum. Res.* 40, 350–367.

Kinsella, H., 2011. *The Image before the weapon: a critical history of the distinction between combatant and civilian.* Cornell University Press, Ithaca.

Kinzler, K. D., Dupoux, E., Spelke, E. S., 2007. The native language of social cognition. *Proc. Natl. Acad. Sci.* 104, 12577–12580.

Klotz, A., 1995. *Norms in international relations: the struggle against apartheid.* Cornell University Press, Ithaca.

Kowert, P., Shannon, V.P., 2012. *Psychology and constructivism in international relations: an ideational alliance.* University of Michigan Press, Ann Arbor.

Kratochwil, F., Ruggie, J. G., 1986. International organization: a state of the art on an art of the state. *Int. Organ.* 40, 753–775.

Krebs, R. R., Jackson, P. T., 2016. Twisting tongues and twisting arms: the power of political rhetoric. *Eur. J. Int. Relat.* 13, 35–66.

Kreps, S., Maxey, S., 2018. Mechanisms of morality: sources of support for humanitarian intervention. *J. Confl. Resolut.* 62, 1814–1842.

Lee, S., Feeley, T. H., 2016. The identifiable victim effect: a meta-analytic review. *Soc. Influ.* 11, 199–215.

Levitin, D. J., 2014. *The organized mind: thinking straight in the age of information overload.* Dutton, New York.

Linde, R., 2016. *The globalization of childhood: the international diffusion of norms and law against the child death penalty.* Oxford University Press.

Mackie, G., 1996. Ending footbinding and infibulation: a convention account. *Am. Sociol. Rev.* 61, 999–1017.

Marcus, G., 2004. *The birth of the mind: how a tiny number of genes creates the complexities of human thought.* Basic Books, New York.

Mattern, J. B., 2011. A practice theory of emotion for International Relations, in Adler, E., Pouliot, V. (eds.), *International practices.* Cambridge University Press, pp. 63–86.

McDermott, R., 2009. Mutual interests: the case for increasing dialogue between political science and neuroscience. *Polit. Res. Q.* 62, 571–583.

McDermott, R., 2004a. *Political psychology in international relations.* University of Michigan Press, Ann Arbor.

McDermott, R., 2004b. The feeling of rationality: the meaning of neuroscientific advances for political science. *Perspect. Polit.* 2, 691–706.

Mcdermott, R., Hatemi, P. K., 2014. The study of international politics in the neurobiological revolution: a review of leadership and political violence. *Millenn. – J. Int. Stud.* 43, 92–123.

McDermott, R., Lopez, A., 2012. Psychology and constructivism: uneasy bedfellows? in *Psychology and constructivism in international relations: an ideological alliance.* University of Michigan Press, Ann Arbor.

Mendos, L. R., 2019. *State-sponsored homophobia 2019: global legislation overview update*. ILGA, Geneva.

Mercer, J., 2014. Feeling like a state: social emotion and identity. *Int. Theory* 6, 515–535.

Mercer, J., 2010. Emotional beliefs. *Int. Organ.* 64, 1–31.

Mercer, J., 1995. Anarchy and identity. *Int. Organ.* 49, 229–252.

Mercier, H., Sperber, D., 2017. *The enigma of reason*. Harvard University Press, Cambridge, MA.

Milgram, S., 2009. *Obedience to authority: an experimental view*, Perennial classic. HarperPerennial/ModernThought, New York.

Miller, E. K., Cohen, J.D., 2001. An integrative theory of prefrontal cortex function. *Annu. Rev. Neurosci.* 24, 167–202.

Moll, J., Zahn, R., Oliveira-Souza, R. D., Krueger, F., Grafman, J., 2005. Opinion: the neural basis of human moral cognition. *Nat. Rev. Neurosci.* 6, 799–809.

Mueller, J.E., 1996. *Retreat from doomsday: the obsolescence of major war*. University of Rochester Press, Rochester, NY.

Nabi, R. L., Gustafson, A., Jensen, R., 2018. Framing climate change: exploring the role of emotion in generating advocacy behavior. *Sci. Commun.* 40, 442–468.

Nadelmann, E. A., 1990. Global prohibition regimes: the evolution of norms in international society. *Int. Organ.* 44, 479–526.

Narvaez, D., 2010. Moral complexity: the fatal attraction of truthiness and the importance of mature moral functioning. *Perspect. Psychol. Sci.* 5, 163–181.

Neuman, W., 2007. *The affect effect: dynamics of emotion in political thinking and behavior*. University of Chicago Press: Chicago.

Oxley, D. R., Smith, K. B., Alford, J. R., et al, 2008. Political attitudes vary with physiological traits. *Science* 321, 1667.

Perrin, S., Spencer, C., 1980. The Asch effect: a child of its time? *Bull. Brit. Psych. Soc.* 33, 405-406.

Pinker, S., 2011. *The better angels of our nature: why violence has declined*, Viking, New York.

Pinker, S., 2008. The moral instinct. *N. Y. Times Mag.*

Pinker, S., 2002. *The blank slate: the modern denial of human nature*. Viking, New York.

Poldrack, R.A., 2018. *The new mind readers: what neuroimaging can and cannot reveal about our thoughts*. Princeton University Press, Princeton; Oxford.

Price, R., 1998. Reversing the gun sights: transnational civil society targets land mines. *Int. Organ.* 52, 613–644.

Price, R., 1997. *The chemical weapons taboo*. Cornell University Press, Ithaca.

Price, R., 2020. Moral psychology, neuroscience, and non-combatant immunity, *European Review of International Studies*. 7, 203–226

Rathbun, B. C., Stein, R., 2019. Greater goods: morality and attitudes toward the use of nuclear weapons. *J. Confl. Resolut.* 64, 002200271987999–816.

Rifkin, J., 2009. *The empathic civilization: the race to global consciousness in a world in crisis*. J.P. Tarcher/Penguin, New York.

Risse, T., 2000. "Let's argue!": communicative action in world politics. *Int. Organ.* 54, 1–39.

Ruggie, J. G., 1982. International regimes, transactions, and change: embedded liberalism in the postwar economic order. *Int. Organ.* 36, 379–415.

Ryan, T. J., 2014. Reconsidering moral issues in politics. *J. Polit.* 76, 380–397.

Schelling, T. C., 1968. The life you save may be your own, in Chase, S. B. (ed.), *Problems in public expenditure analysis*. The Brookings Institution, Washington, DC, pp. 127–161.

Schmidt, A., Sikkink, K., 2019. Breaking the ban? the heterogeneous impact of US contestation of the torture norm. *J. Glob. Secur. Stud.* 4, 105–122.

Schwartz, S. H., 2012. An overview of the Schwartz theory of basic values. *Online Read. Psychol. Cult.* 2.

Schwartz, S. H., Caprara, G. V., Vecchione, M., 2010. Basic personal values, core political values, and voting: a longitudinal analysis. *Polit. Psychol.* 31, 421–452.

Semenova, N. S., Kiseleva, E. V., Ilyashevich, M. V., Alisievich, E. S., 2015. Traditional values and human rights of LGBTI in the framework of the UN and Council of Europe: international legal aspects. *Mediterr. J. Soc. Sci.* 6, 315–324.

Shannon, V.P., 2012. Introduction, in *Psychology and constructivism in international relations: an ideational alliance*. University of Michigan Press, Ann Arbor, pp. 1–29.

Sikkink, K., 2011. *The justice cascade: how human rights prosecutions are changing world politics*. WW Norton & Co., New York.

Sikkink, K., 1986. Codes of conduct for transnational corporations: the case of the WHO/UNICEF code. *Int. Organ.* 40, 815–840.

Simmons, B., 2009. *Mobilizing for human rights: international law and domestic politics*. Cambridge University Press, New York.

Singer, P., 1972. Famine, affluence, and morality. *Phil and Public Affairs* 1, 229–243.

Singer, P., 2011. *The expanding circle: ethics, evolution, and moral progress*. Princeton University Press, Princeton, NJ.

Singer, T., Klimecki, O. M., 2014. Empathy and compassion. *Curr. Biol.* 24, R875–R878.

Sinnott-Armstrong, W., 2007. Introduction, in Sinnott-Armstrong, W. (ed.), *Moral psychology: the neuroscience of morality: emotion, brain disorders, and development*, The MIT Press Series. MIT Press, Cambridge, MA.

Sinnott-Armstrong, W., Young, L., Cushman, F., 2010. Moral intuitions, in *The moral psychology handbook*. Oxford University Press, Oxford, UK, 246–272.

Sloman, S. A., Fernbach, P., 2017. *The knowledge illusion: why we never think alone*. Riverhead Books, New York.

Slovic, P., Västfjäll, D., Erlandsson, A., Gregory, R., 2017. Iconic photographs and the ebb and flow of empathic response to humanitarian disasters. *Proc. Natl. Acad. Sci. U. S. A.* 114, 640–644.

Slovic, P., Västfjäll, D., Gregory, R., Giusti Olson, K., 2016. Valuing lives you might save: understanding psychic numbing in the face of genocide, in Anderton, C., Brauer, J. (eds.), *Economic aspects of genocides, other mass atrocities, and their prevention*. Oxford University Press, pp. 613–638.

Small, D. A., Loewenstein, G., Slovic, P., 2007. Sympathy and callousness: The impact of deliberative thought on donations to identifiable and statistical victims. *Organ. Behav. Hum. Decis. Process.* 102, 143–153.

Smetana, M., Vranka, M., 2020. How moral foundations shape public approval of nuclear, chemical, and conventional strikes: new evidence from experimental surveys. *International Interactions*.

Stein, J., 1988. Building politics into psychology: the misperception of threat. *Pol. Psychol.* 9, 245–271.

Stein, J., 2017. The micro-foundations of international relations theory: psychology and behavioral economics. *Int. Organ.* 71, S249–S263.

Stensvold, A. (ed.), 2016. *Religion, state and the United Nations: value politics*. Routledge.

Stolerman, D., Lagnado, D., 2018. The moral foundations of human rights attitudes. *Polit. Psychol.*

Tetlock, P. E., 1983. Psychological research on foreign policy: a methodological overview. *Rev. Personal. Soc. Psychol.* 4, 45–79.

Tetlock, P. E., Kristel, O. V., Elson, S. B., Green, M. C., Lerner, J.S., 2000. The psychology of the unthinkable: taboo trade-offs, forbidden base rates, and heretical counterfactuals. *J. Pers. Soc. Psychol.* 78, 853–870.

Thalhammer, K. E., 2007. *Courageous resistance: the power of ordinary people*, Palgrave Macmillan, New York.

Tingley, D., 2011. Neurological imaging and the evaluation of competing theories, in *Biology and politics: the cutting edge*. Emerald Group Publishing, pp. 187–204.

Tingley, D., 2006. Evolving political science. *Polit. Life Sci.* 25, 23–41.

Towns, A. E., 2010. *Women and states: norms and hierarchies in international society.* Cambridge University Press, Cambridge; New York.

Traven, D., 2015. Moral cognition and the law and ethics of armed conflict. *Int. Stud. Rev.* 17, 556–587.

Tversky, A., Kahneman, D., 1973. Availability: a heuristic for judging frequency and probability. *Cognit. Psychol.* 5, 207–232.

UN Human Rights Council Advisory Committee, 2012. Study of the Human Rights Council Advisory Committee on Promoting Human Rights and Fundamental Freedoms Through a Better Understanding of Traditional Values of Humankind.

United Nations Human Rights Council Resolution 21/3, 2012. Promoting human rights and fundamental freedoms through a better understanding of traditional values of humankind:, A/HRC/RES/21/3. UN.

United Nations Office of the High Commissioner for Human Rights, 2021. www.ohchr.org/EN/ProfessionalInterest/Pages/CMW.aspx

Verweij, M., Senior, T. J., Dominguez D., J. F., Turner, R., 2015. Emotion, rationality, and decision-making: how to link affective and social neuroscience with social theory. *Front. Neurosci.* 9, 332.

Vosoughi, S., Roy, D., Aral, S., 2018. The spread of true and false news online. *Sci. Am. Assoc. Adv. Sci.* 359, 1146–1151.

Warneken, F., Tomasello, M., 2006. Altruistic helping in human infants and young chimpanzees. *Science* 311, 1301–1303.

Watson, J. C., Greenberg, L. S., 2009. Empathic resonance: a neuroscience perspective, in *The social neuroscience of empathy.* MIT Press, pp. 125–37.

Watson, S., 2009. *The securitization of humanitarian migration: digging moats and sinking boats.* Routledge, London; New York.

Weiss, M. L., 2013. Prejudice before pride: rise of an anticipatory countermovement in Global homophobia: states, movements, and the politics of oppression. University of Illinois Press, Urbana, IL.

Wendt, A., 1999. *Social theory of international politics.* Cambridge University Press, Cambridge.

Wexler, B. E., 2006. *Brain and culture: neurobiology, ideology, and social change.* MIT Press, Cambridge, MA.

Wiener, A., 2014. *A theory of contestation.* Springer.

Wong, S. S., 2016. Emotions and the communication of intentions in face-to-face diplomacy. *Eur. J. Int. Relat.* 22, 144–167.

Yehuda, R., Daskalakis, N. P., Bierer, L. M., et al., 2016. Holocaust exposure induced intergenerational effects on FKBP5 methylation. *Biol. Psychiatry* 80, 372–380

Cambridge Elements ☰

# International Relations

## Series Editors

### Jon C. W. Pevehouse
*University of Wisconsin–Madison*

Jon C. W. Pevehouse is the Vilas Distinguished Achievement Professor of Political Science at the University of Wisconsin–Madison. He has published numerous books and articles in IR in the fields of international political economy, international organizations, foreign policy analysis, and political methodology. He is a former editor of the leading IR field journal, International Organization.

### Tanja A. Börzel
*Freie Universität Berlin*

Tanja A. Börzel is the Professor of political science and holds the Chair for European Integration at the Otto-Suhr-Institute for Political Science, Freie Universität Berlin. She holds a PhD from the European University Institute, Florence, Italy. She is coordinator of the Research College "The Transformative Power of Europe," as well as the FP7-Collaborative Project "Maximizing the Enlargement Capacity of the European Union" and the H2020 Collaborative Project "The EU and Eastern Partnership Countries: An Inside-Out Analysis and Strategic Assessment." She directs the Jean Monnet Center of Excellence "Europe and its Citizens."

### Edward D. Mansfield
*University of Pennsylvania*

Edward D. Mansfield is the Hum Rosen Professor of Political Science, University of Pennsylvania. He has published well over 100 books and articles in the area of international political economy, international security, and international organizations. He is Director of the Christopher H. Browne Center for International Politics at the University of Pennsylvania and former program co-chair of the American Political Science Association.

## Associate Editors

Jeffrey T. Checkel European University Institute

Miles Kahler American University

# Cambridge Elements ≡

# International Relations

Printed in the United States
by Baker & Taylor Publisher Services
Printed in the United States
by Baker & Taylor Publisher Services